5000 YEARS OF CHINESE COSTUMES

5000 YEARS OF CHINESE COSTUMES

Text:
Zhou Xun, Gao Chunming
Editing:
The Chinese Costumes Research Group of the
Shanghai School of Traditional Operas

THE COMMERCIAL PRESS

This book is the recipient of the following awards:

1) The Best Produced Book in Hong Kong (1984), sponsored by Urban Council, Hong Kong.

2) Award of Excellence for Book Design, CA-84, 25th Annual Exhibition sponsored by Communication Arts Magazine, U.S.A.

3) Bronze Medal for "Best Designed Books From All Over the World in 1984", competition held in Leipzig, East Germany.

5000 YEARS OF CHINESE COSTUMES

© 1984, 1987 The Commercial Press (H.K.) Ltd. · Academia Press

Chinese edition first published March 1984
Third Impression July 1998
English edition first published August 1987
Second Impression July 1998
by The Commercial Press (H.K.) Ltd.

Edited by: The Chinese Costumes Research Group of
 the Shanghai School of Traditional Operas
Written by: Zhou Xun, Gao Chunming

Executive Editors (Chinese Edition) : Wong Kong Sang, Shen Zhaorong
 (English Edition) : Eastre Tsui-Yee Tang
Arts Editor: Wan Yat Sha
Reconstructed Drawings by: Zhou Xun, Gao Chunming,
 Zou Zhenya, Liu Yuemei
Photographs by: Zhou Zuyi, Jin Baoyuan
Graphic Design by: S S Design & Production

Printed in Hong Kong by
C & C Offset Printing Co., Ltd.

All rights reserved. No part of this publication may be reproduced, stored in a retrieval system, or transmitted in any form or by any means, electronic, mechanical, photocopying, recording and/or otherwise without the prior written permission of the publishers.

ISBN 962 07 5055 1

FOREWORD

In talking about costume museum, the late Prime Minister Zhou En-lai had raised a question in 1964 asking if it is possible to edit a pictorial book on costumes as we Chinese have such a long history and a lot of old and new materials. I personally feel that this volume of "5000 Years of Chinese Costumes" is really a masterpiece which can serve as a basic reference for the construction of a costume museum for China.

Professor **Zhao Jingshen**
Fudan University China

(extract from Wenhui Bao 1984.5.12)

This album includes the styles, patterns, colour matching and all the beauty of Chinese costumes in different dynasties of 5000 years.

There are a great number of colourful reconstructed drawings and pictures of costume parts ranging from headgear, clothing to shoes which are extremely exquisite and very useful to people working in our field (art and design) in stimulating ideas for creation.

Mr. **Yu Zhenfei**
Vice chairman
China Federation of Literary & Art Cirles

(extract from Renmin Ribao 1984.6.6.)

CONTENTS

Foreword   5

Tables of Contents of Illustrations   7

Introduction   9

1. Ancient Times   10
2. Qin and Han Dynasties   30
3. Wei, Jin and the Southern and Northern Dynasties   52
4. Sui, Tang and the Five Dynasties   74
5. Song Dynasty   104
6. Liao, Jin and Yuan Dynasties   128
7. Ming Dynasty   144
8. Qing Dynasty   170
9. Modern Times   212

Appendices

I. Summary Table of Evolution of Costume   244
II. Illustrations Indicating Specific Parts of Costumes   246
III. Table Showing Measurements of Spread Illustrations of Costumes   250
IV. Bibliography   252
V. Index of Figures   253

TABLE OF CONTENTS OF ILLUSTRATIONS

*Ancient Times

1.	Primitive Clothing and Accessories	14
2.	Hairstyles and Headdresses of the Shang Dynasty	15
3.	Clothing and Accessories of Nobility in Shang and Zhou Dynasties	18
4.	Men's Costume of the Zhou Dynasty	19
5.	Straight Unlined Garment	23
6.	Jacket and Trousers	24
7.	Spiral-shaped One-piece Garment	25
8.	Armour and 'Hu Fu'	28

*Qin and Han Dynasties

1.	Emperor's 'Mian Guan', 'Mian Fu' and 'Chi Xi'	34
2.	Men's Robe	36
3.	Spiral-shaped One-piece Garment	38
4.	Wound-lapel One-piece Garment	41
5.	Women's Straight Robe	43
6.	Women's Jacket and Skirt	44
7.	Female Dancer's Costume	45
8.	Armour	47

*Wei, Jin and the Southern and Northern Dynasties

1.	Lacquered Gauze Cage Hat and Loose Gown with Large Sleeves	56
2.	'Ku Zhe'	61
3.	Women's Multi-lap Swallowtail Costume	62
4.	Women's Unlined Upper Garment and Skirt	65
5.	Costumes and Adornments of the Common People	68
6.	Helmet and Armour	70
7.	Fabrics	73

*Sui, Tang and the Five Dynasties

1.	Emperor's Costumes and Accessories	78
2.	Civil Officials' Ceremonial Dresses	79
3.	'Fu Tou' and Robes	81
4.	Women's Hairstyles	84
5.	Women's Makeup and Adornments	86
6.	Jacket and Skirt, Short-sleeved Upper Garment and Cape	88
7.	'Hu Fu'	93
8.	Large-sleeved Gown	94
9.	Costumes and Adornments of Female Dancers	96
10.	'Hui Hu' Costume	98
11.	Armour	100

*Song Dynasty

1.	Emperor's Court Dress	108
2.	Empress' Ceremonial Dress	110
3.	Formal Dress for Officials	111
4.	Costumes for Scholars	112
5.	Broad-sleeved Garment	115
6.	Over-dress	119
7.	Jacket and Skirt	121
8.	Costumes of the Common People	124
9.	Armour	126

*Liao, Jin and Yuan Dynasties

1.	Costumes of the Liao Dynasty	132
2.	Costumes of the Jin Dynasty	136
3.	Gold Brocade Dragon Robe	138
4.	Square Corrugated Hat and Plaited Garment	140
5.	Costumes for Aristocratic Women	141
6.	Jacket and Skirt and Half Sleeve Over-jacket	142

*Ming Dynasty

1.	Emperor's Ordinary Dress	148
2.	Empress' Ceremonial Dress	150
3.	Ordinary Wear for Officials	152
4.	Ordinary Dress for Noblemen	156
5.	Costumes and Accessories for Scholars	159
6.	Jacket and Skirt	161
7.	Over-dress and Sleeveless Over-dress	164
8.	Paddy-field Design Dress	167
9.	Armour	168

*Qing Dynasty

1.	Emperor's Costumes and Accessories	174
2.	Empress' Costumes and Accessories	178
3.	Costumes and Accessories for Officials	182
4.	Men's Ordinary Wear	191
5.	Ceremonial Dress of Titled Ladies	194
6.	Dresses of Women of Han Nationality	195
7.	Costumes of Women of Manchu Nationality	199
8.	Armour	200
9.	Stage Costumes	202
10.	Costumes and Accessories of the Taiping Heavenly Kingdom	203
11.	Fabrics and Decorative Borders	210

*Modern Times

1.	Men's Costumes	216
2.	Women's Hairstyles	217
3.	Lined Upper Garment and Skirt	221
4.	Evolution of 'Qi Pao'	228
5.	Women's Fashions in the 1930's	236
6.	Costumes of the Common People	238
7.	Jewellery	240

INTRODUCTION

China is a country with a long history and an ancient civilisation, and has sometimes been called "the Kingdom of Costumes and Headgear". Throughout the long years of Chinese history the Chinese people have created many colourful and artistic styles of costume. Costume has always been a brilliant feature of Chinese civilisation.

Unfortunately, since garments and accessories are not easy to preserve, few of them have survived to the present day. And although descriptions of dress can be found in the historical records of various dynasties, detailed descriptions exist only of items that were in the wardrobes of emperors, kings and officials. The dress of the common people was either mentioned only briefly or ignored completely. Moreover, the records were seldom, if ever, supported by illustrations, so that it is very hard for us to picture ancient modes of dress in their entirety.

In China, dress has always been an inseparable part of cultural history, and it can be related to politics, ideology, military history, economics, culture and the arts. The aim of this volume is to trace the historical development of Chinese costume, to show how it is related to the social customs and ways of life during different historical periods and to provide materials for the study of Chinese history. We hope that such an account, besides being of interest to the general reader, will be of use to professionals in the fields of costume design, fine art, drama, cinema and literature.

The arrangement is chronological and the book is divided into nine sections: Ancient times; Qin and Han; Wei, Jin and the Southern and Northern Dynasties; Sui, Tang and the Five Dynasties; Song; Liao, Jin and Yuan; Ming; Qing; Modern times. The main sources are historical records, both official and unofficial, and the personal notes of scholars. Considerable space is devoted to items of dress displayed in museums in different parts of the country, and to such evidence as pottery figurines, frescoes, sculptures, stone carvings and famous paintings. The purpose is to introduce the reader to the various forms of dress worn by people of different classes and regional groups in each period.

One way to gain an impression of the styles, patterns and colours of Chinese costume is to examine human figures and artistic patterns in paintings and other historical relics such as inscriptions on ancient bronzes and stone tablets, frescoes and clay figurines and carvings in brick and stone. We have made extensive use of such materials to reconstruct the distinctive features of the costume of different periods and to make facsimile drawings. So far as we know this approach has not been used before in the history of Chinese costume. We would welcome readers' comments on this method.

Given China's long history and vast area, it is obviously impossible to present in one volume a complete history of Chinese costume, which has many social and regional variations, as well as those associated with historical change. It is necessary therefore to be selective and to concentrate on the major aspects. Whilst we have endeavoured to make our selection as comprehensive and as representative as possible, there may well be disagreement over our choice. On this, too, we would welcome readers' comments. It must be recognised, however, that much research remains to be done in this field, and that many important points will only emerge as further historical data are unearthed.

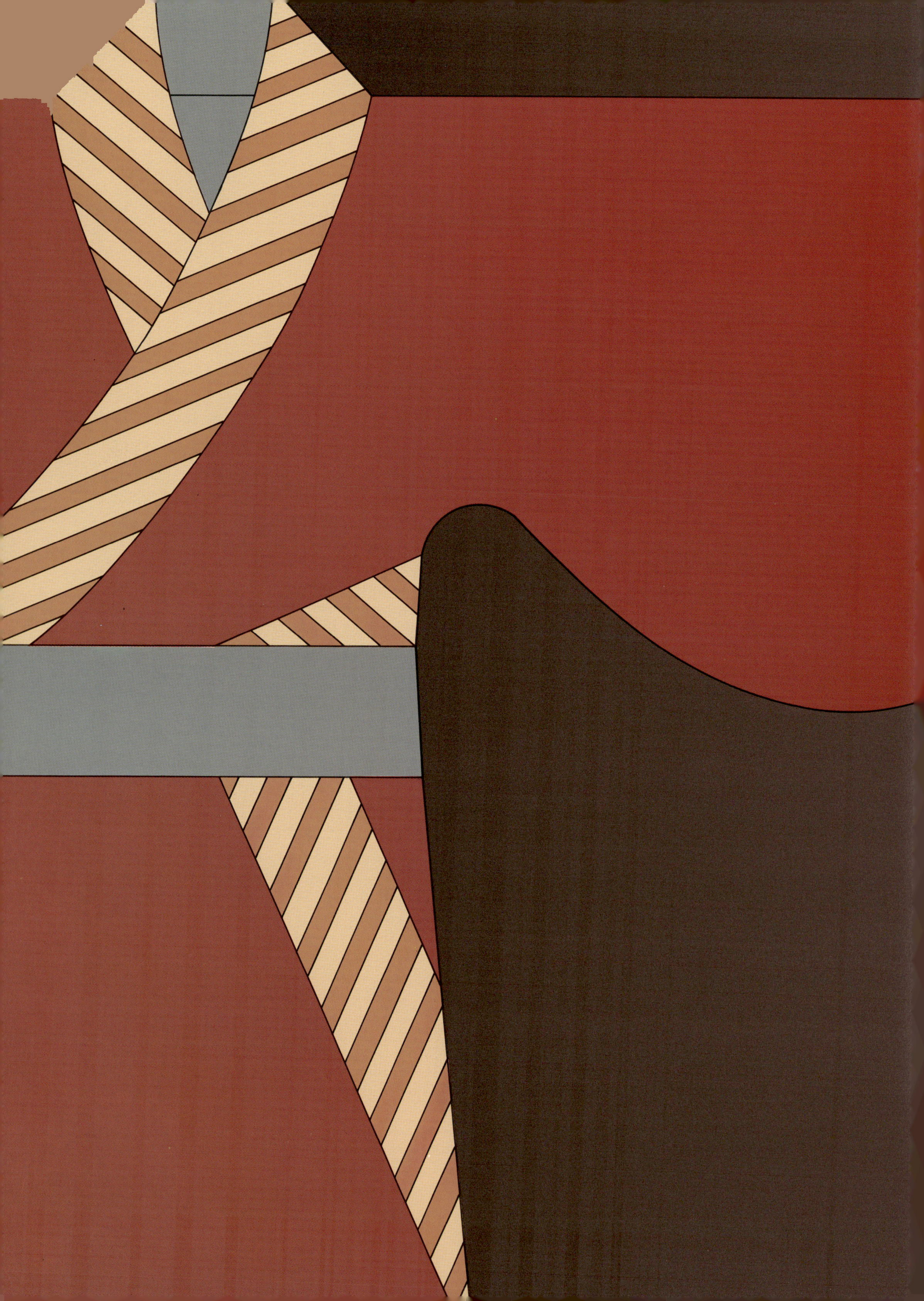

上古

ANCIENT TIMES

In the earliest times, human beings dwelt in caves in densely forested mountains. Their way of life was primitive, and for clothing they had nothing but leaves and grass. Eventually, however, they discovered that furs could be used for protection against the cold, and they began to wrap themselves in animal skins.

In the last phase of the Old Stone Age, Peking Man inhabited the hilltop of Zhoukoudian, in what is now the south-western district of Beijing; Zhiyu Man lived in what is now Su County, Shaanxi Province; and Hutouliang Man lived in Yangyuan County, Hebei Province. Among the remains dug up in caves where these primitive people once lived needles made of animal bone have been found, providing evidence that several tens of thousands of years ago the art of sewing was known, and people were able to make simple stitches. They stripped the skin from animals and sewed the pelt into clothes for protection against severe cold. The emergence of such primitive clothing is a curtain-raiser to the history of costume. Though it is now agreed that clothing serves other important purposes, such as covering the genitals and providing adornment, protection from cold must have been the primary consideration in prehistoric times.

By about 4,000 B. C. — 3,000 B. C. matriarchal communities in China's primitive society had reached a stage of prosperity and primitive agriculture and handicrafts began to develop. These early people took the fibres of hemp and, using stone or earthenware spindles, twisted them into threads, which they then wove into hemp cloth to make clothes. The development from wrapping the body in skins to sewing clothes from sackcloth marked a major step forward in human progress.

As China was the first country to develop agriculture, the Chinese were preeminent in this field of technology. By the Shang Dynasty, the Chinese people had already mastered the skill of silk weaving, and had even made improvements to looms and invented facilities for jacquard weaving which enabled them to produce exquisitely beautiful silk fabric. By stages embroidery and dyeing also emerged, providing a solid basis for the development of the arts of silk weaving, embroidery and dyeing that followed in the ensuing several thousand years.

In ancient times men did not cut their hair. Only offenders had their hair and beard cut off — a form of punishment known as *kun shou*. Ordinarily a man would allow his hair to hang down over his shoulders. Later, however, this was found to be rather inconvenient, and men began to tie their hair with strings. Some even worked animal bones or jade to some symmetrical shape, fastened strings to them, and used them on their heads both to hold the hair in place and for decoration.

In the Shang Dynasty men usually wore their hair in a long queue, or pigtail, though some wore a cap or turban. The custom of wearing headgear, which began in the Shang Dynasty, became popular in the following Zhou Dynasty. From examples of Zhou Dynasty figurines in jade, stone, pottery and bronze it can be seen that virtually all men at that time wore caps and very few went bareheaded.

The turbans or caps of the Shang Dynasty were usually wraps made of silk or cloth. In the Zhou Dynasty there also appeared other kinds of cap that were flat, or crescent-shaped, or bulging in the middle and curling in at the sides. The low, flat styles were usually worn by commoners, while the tall, pointed types were the monopoly of men of high birth.

Women's hairstyles in the Shang Dynasty were only slightly different from men's. Their queues were generally wavy and hung down over the shoulders. Some women, however, preferred to wear caps. Relics of the period show that women wore hair ornaments such as bone pins. Women's hairstyles remained basically unchanged up to the Spring and Autumn and Warring States Period, though customs varied from place to place. Some made their plait into an enormous bun hanging down at the back of the neck, while others dressed their hair into two large braids, hanging down over the breasts. Some, after arranging their hair into a braid, added false hair to the end so that it flowed down to the knees.

China's dress system was founded somewhere in the period of the Xia and the Shang Dynasties, and was perfected in the Zhou Dynasty as an instrument of rulers to identify status and demonstrate authority. The highborn and the lowly, the noble and the humble, were differentiated in this way. Through in the Spring and Autumn and Warring States Period, the code for dress and headgear was gradually brought within the framework of 'rule by rites', and became one of the manifestations of etiquette and ceremony. Subsequently the dress system for emperors, kings, empresses, queens, imperial concubines, nobles and officials was further elaborated, making the rank system increasingly specific.

According to the regulations laid down in the "Book of Rites of Zhou", emperors, kings and all officials participating in the rites had to wear ceremonial costumes consisting of a crown or cap, *xian yi* (black clothes) and *xiu shang* (embroidered trousers). The most dignified ceremonial headgear was *mian guan*, worn only on the occasion of rites attended by emperors, kings and officials. This explains the use of the idiom *guan mian tang huang*, meaning very impressive-looking, to describe someone's composure. According to the regulations, those who wore *mian guan* were obliged also to wear *mian fu* (sacrificial robes); these were different for the upper and lower classes, and the colours and designs — traditionally called *zhang wen* (decorative patterns) — were never the same. The emperor's *mian fu*, for example, was *xian yi yin shang* (a black coat and red trousers). The coat was decorated with motifs representing the sun, the moon, stars, mountains, dragons and phoenixes. The trousers were ornamented with six embroidered motifs: *zong yi* alga, fire, rice, figures of axes and *fu*.

Each of the patterns had its own significance: sun, moon and stars stood for radiance, mountains for stability, dragons for quick decisions, and phoenixes for gaiety and colour. *Zong yi* was a ritual article (later it contained also a tiger and a longtailed monkey, standing for loyalty and filial piety. Alga stood for cleanliness, fire for brightness, rice for nutrition, the axe for decisiveness and *fu*, a decorative texture of black and blue, (either in the shape of the Chinese character "亞" or with two beasts back to back) for judgement. Thus on the most solemn occasions the emperor wore a costume bearing no less than twelve motifs, but the number decreased with the diminishing importance of the occasion. The same applied to the jade strings on the emperor's crown or cap. When there were nine strings, the coat and trousers bore seven motifs; when there were seven strings, the coat and trousers bore five motifs, and so on. Dukes, princes, ministers and other officials were also present at ritual ceremonies, and if the emperor's costume was decorated with twelve motifs, dukes had to have nine, marquises and earls seven, and so on, with the number of motifs diminishing in accordance with diminishing rank. This then was the basic regulation for the sacrificial rites.

For empresses, there were six designated forms of dress *wei yi, yu zhi, qu zhi, ju yi, zhen yi* and *tuan yi*. The first three were worn in the company of the emperor at sacrificial rites. *Ju yi* was the costume worn when attending *qin can* (a prayer ritual to report the sericulture and silk production situation of the past year to the deceased emperor). *Zhen yi* was worn when seeing the emperor formally or when holding banquets. *Tuan yi* was a form of casual wear. There were also detailed regulations concerning the clothing of all women of rank, according to their status.

The typical costume of this period was the two-piece garment. The coat had to be in one of the 'stately' colours: blue, red, yellow, white or black, while the trousers were some mixture of these colours. The costumes of the Shang and Zhou Dynasties generally had narrow sleeves and the coats were long enough to reach the knees. Along the collar, sleeves and hems there were borders of various designs, and the coat was tied around the waist with a girdle.

In the Warring States Period drastic changes in dress and ornaments took place, the most important being the popularization of *hu fu* — the dress of a national minority in the northwest of China. Generally speaking this comprised a short jacket, long trousers and leather boots, the jacket being tight-fitting to allow greater freedom of movement. The first person to adopt this kind of clothing was King Wuling of the State of Zhao, the earliest reformist in the annals of Chinese costume. His adoption of the apparel of the northern tribal nomads and introduction of their horse-back archery were in tune with the needs of warfare, and contributed to the increase in power and prosperity of his state. From then on, *hu fu* was widely worn throughout China, and became the general fashion for that era.

Towards the end of the Spring and Autumn Period and the beginning of the Warring States Period, there appeared another kind of costume known as *shen yi*. Unlike the preceeding costume, this was a one-piece robe, whose popularity had important repercussions on the society of that period. Both men and women, and officials and military officers alike, all took up this fashion.

Footwear in ancient times included *lu* (shoes), *xi* (high-class shoes), *ju* (walking shoes), *jue* (ordinary shoes), *xie* and *xue* (boots). *Lu* is the general term for shoes, and can be applied to any of the shoes worn with ceremonial costume. *Xi* were the most sophisticated kind of shoes. In the Zhou Dynasty, *Xi* worn by emperors were of three colours: white, black and red. Those worn by empresses were red, blue or black. On the most solemn occasions emperors wore red shoes, while empresses wore black, in both cases made of satin. The chief difference between *xi* and other kinds of footwear was that they had wooden soles to prevent the uppers from getting wet. *Ju* were a kind of shoe made for everyday wear out of materials like hemp. They generally had thin soles, and were worn by officials at home. If they went out, they wore *jue*, which were made from sandal straw. These were light and convenient, suitable for walking. *Xie* were ordinary shoes with high heels, originally made from sheepskin, and later of silk and hemp as well, hence the alternative name 'silk shoes' and 'hemp shoes'. As for the boots, they originated in the western region, as part of *hu fu*. When *hu fu* became popular, Han people also began to wear boots.

Two different kinds of armour were worn in ancient times: leather mail, and cloth mail. Shortly after the establishment of the Zhou Dynasty, bronze and iron armour appeared also.

1. Primitive Clothing and Accessories

Prior to the manufacture of textiles, men skinned captured animals and used the tendons as threads to sew the animals' pelt into clothes. Among the animals most often hunted were red deer, spotted deer, wild oxen, antelopes, foxes, badgers and rabbits.

Among the remains of Hilltop Cave Man and some ancient tombs, many ornamental relics have been found, including ornaments for the head, neck and wrists. They were made of beautiful natural stones, animals' teeth, fish bones, or the shells of sea or river clams and freshwater mussels. People probably wore these ornaments not just for decoration, but also to commemorate their exploits in fishing or hunting.

Fig. 1 Primitive clothing and necklace — a drawing based on ancient texts, and primitive tailoring tools such as bone needles and awls found in excavations.

Ancient Times 15

2. Hairstyles and Headdresses of the Shang Dynasty

In the Yin ruins, site of the capital of the Shang Dynasty in its later period and situated in what is now the northwestern outskirts of Anyang City in Henan Province, archaeologists found a large number of jade objects. Among these were many quite graceful human images, each with a characteristic hairstyle and clothing which reflect to a certain extent the social customs of the time.

From these jade figurines, it can be seen that the braids worn by men of the Shang Dynasty were of different styles. One method used was to gather the hair to the top of the head, plait it into a queue and let it hang down behind. Another was to comb and plait the hair on either side with the ends of the braid curled up and hanging down over the shoulders. Still another was to plait the hair into a braid and coil it up at the top. Men of higher rank, however, wore turbans or caps decorated with beautiful geometric designs.

Women's hairstyles also had their own features. From ornaments such as the emeralds preserved at the Imperial Palace Museum in Beijing, it can be seen that women in those early days wore hairpins. According to the etiquette and customs of the Zhou Dynasty, girls past the age of fifteen and engaged to be married had to go through a hairpin-wearing ceremony to show that they had come of age and already had a fiance. Single women over the age of twenty had to go through a similar ceremony, though the occasion might not be quite so ceremonious and the kinds of hairpins were somewhat different. This custom was so influential that even the Ming and Qing Dynasties' custom "*kai lian shang tou*" (plucking off the fine hair on the face and combing the hair in the manner of a grown-up woman) developed from it.

Most of the numerous hairpins of the Shang Dynasty discovered in ancient tombs were made of animal bones, though some were made of ivory or precious stones. One end of the hairpin was usually decorated with chickens, birds, mandarin ducks or geometric designs; and from ancient literature we learn that such pins were used to distinguish social position not only by women but also by men.

Fig. 2-3 Two views of a braid (Jade figurine from Yin ruins at Anyang, Henan Province)

Fig. 4-5 Shang Dynasty Men, braid coiled up on top (Ceramic figurines believed to be from Yin ruins at Xiaodun in Anyang, Henan Province. Originals now preserved in Taiwan)

16 Ancient Times

Fig. 6 A Shang Dynasty woman wearing a hairpin (A jade ornament preserved in the Imperial Palace Museum, Beijing)

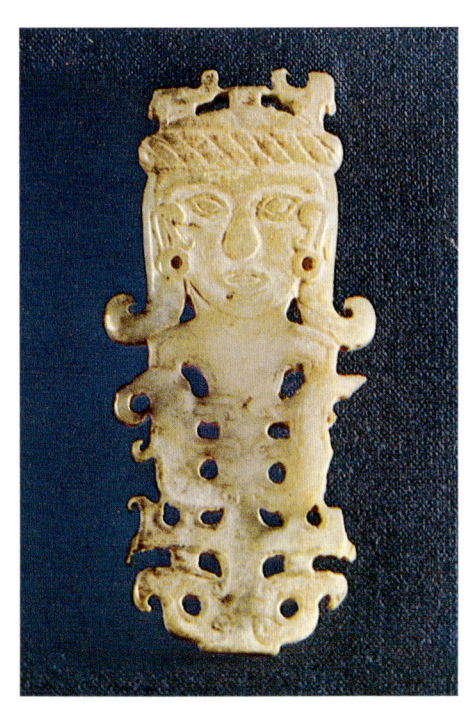

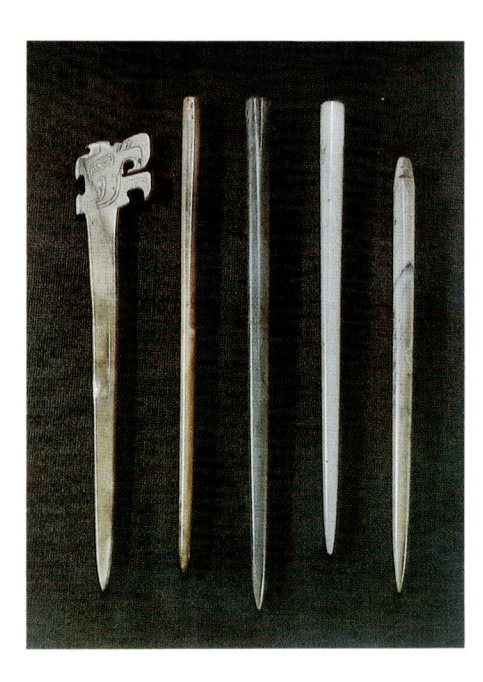

Fig. 7 Jade hairpins of the Shang Dynasty (Relics from the tomb of Fuhau (one of King Wuding's concubines) at Yin ruins in Anyang, Henan Province)

Fig. 8-9 Bone hairpins of the Shang Dynasty (Objects of antiquity in Shanghai Museum)

Ancient Times 17

Fig. 10 A Shang Dynasty man wearing a hairpin (Jade figurine from the tomb of Fuhau at Yin ruins in Anyang, Henan Province)

Fig. 11 Rear view of a Shang Dynasty man wearing a head band (Stone figurine from the tomb of Fuhau at Yin ruins in Anyang, Henan Province)

18 Ancient Times

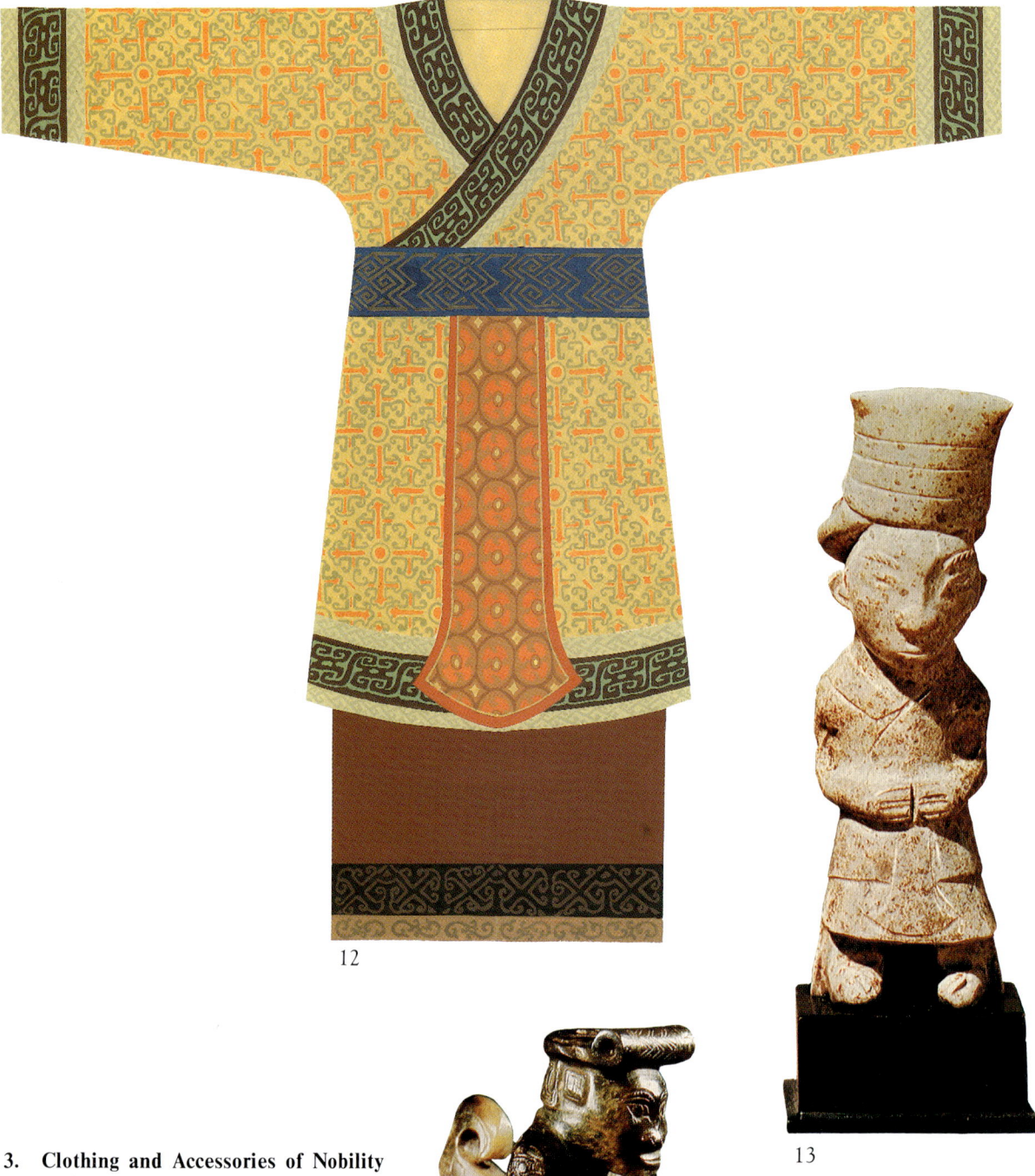

3. Clothing and Accessories of Nobility in Shang and Zhou Dynasties

One of the jade figurines unearthed from the tomb of Fuhau at the Yin ruins in Anyang County, Henan Province, is in the shape of a nobleman wearing a cylindrical turban and elaborate costume. His hair is coiled up on the top of the head under a hoop-shaped ornament, which is actually a cap. His clothes are covered with cloud patterns and at the waist he wears a broad band, the upper part of which presses against the lower part of the collar. The coat covers the knees, and over his belly there is an axe-shaped embroidered ornament narrow at the top and broad at the bottom. This kind of ornament is the precursor of the later *bi xi* (knee cover), but in that period was called *fuo* or *wei bi*.

Fig. 12 Symmetrically tailored garment with narrow sleeves and embroidered axe-shaped ornament (Drawing based on the costume of an unearthed jade figurine)

Fig. 13 Nobleman wearing cylinder-shaped cap and narrowsleeved costume with embroidered axe-shaped ornament (Jade figurine of Western Zhou Dynasty. An antique object, the original now in Furgh Art Gallery, Harvard University, U.S.A.)

Ancient Times 19

4. Men's Costume of the Zhou Dynasty

On the whole clothing and ornamentation of the Zhou Dynasty followed the Shang convention, but there were some minor changes. The clothes were somewhat looser, the sleeves could be either large or small, and the collar was usually rectangular, cut in the shape of a "⊐".

The costume of this period was still worn without buttons, so it was usually tied at the waist by means of a girdle, sometimes accompanied by a jade ornament. The waist bands were of two kinds: one of woven silk called the *da dai* (big girdle) or *shen dai* (scholar's band). When officials went to audiences of the Emperor, the band also served as a kind of tablet held before the breast. That is why later generations called the county nobles or officials *shen shi* (local gentry), meaning that they were qualified to carry such a tablet. The other kind of waist band was made of leather and was called *ge dai* (leather belt), which was for tying the axe-shaped embroidered ornament or for wearing on one's chest.

During the Spring and Autumn Period, especially after the adoption of *hu fu* by Han people, the use of waist bands became more widespread and their workmanship grew even more refined. Gold, silver or pearls were usually set on them for the sake of ornamentation. These bands were called *gou luo dai* (hooked band). The two ends of the band were fastened with hooks. The hooks were called *dai gou* in the language of the Han people but also bore names of foreign origin such as *xian bei, xi pi, shi bi* and *xu bi,* all of which probably originated from the Hu. It was easy to fasten, and gradually superseded the *shen dai*. The *dai gou* were of different sizes and shapes with distinctive features: some as long as one foot, others as short as an inch. It should be mentioned, however, that the *gou luo dai* was not just for tying at the waist, it also served to hold a knife, dagger, sheath, mirror, seal or other ornamental article. After Wei, Jin and the Southern and Northern Dynasties, owing to the introduction of the *die xie dai* (leather waistband), the *gou luo dai* gradually fell into disuse.

Fig. 14 Nobleman wearing cylinder-shaped cap and elaborate garment (Jade figurine from the tomb of Fuhau at Anyang, Yin ruins in Anyang, Henan Province)

Fig. 15 Rectangular collared robe with narrow sleeves (Drawing after reconstruction of a bronze human figure from an unearthed ceramic mould)

Fig. 16 Spread of a symmetrically patterned garment with narrow sleeves (Drawing based on a reconstruction of an unearthed bronze human figure)

Ancient Times 21

17

Fig. 17 Rectangular collared robe with narrow sleeves (Drawing based on reconstruction from a ceramic mould from an Eastern Zhou Dynasty tomb in what is now Houma City, Shaanxi Province)

Fig. 18 Male figure in cap and rectangular collared robe with narrow sleeves (Ceramic mould from an Eastern Zhou Dynasty tomb in Houma City, Shaanxi Province)

18

22   Ancient Times

Fig. 19   A king's bodyguard in rectangular collared outfit with narrow sleeves (Bronze human figure from tomb of the Marquis Zeng in Sui County, Hubei Province)

Fig. 20-22   Gold and silver interlocking hooks (Antique article. Original now in the Shanghai Museum)

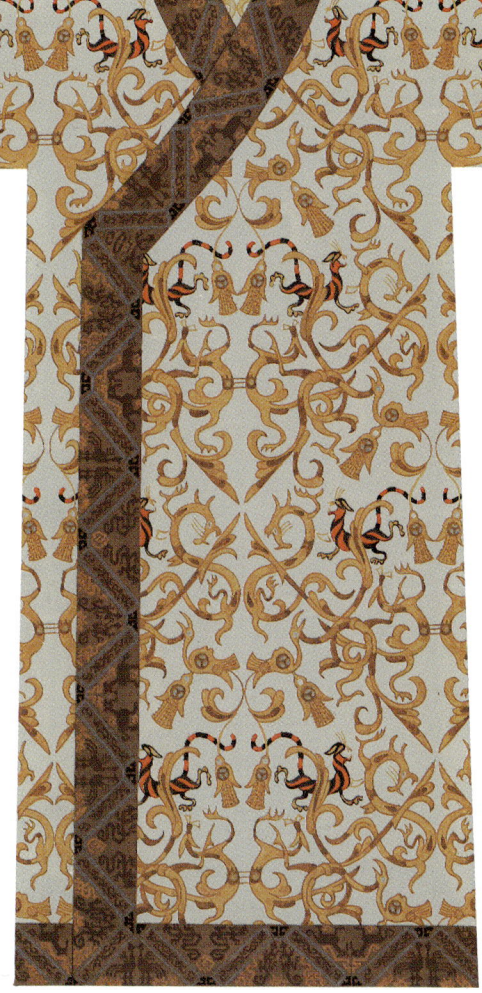

Fig. 23 Embroidered silk gauze unlined garment (Copied from photograph of the original found in Horse Brick No. 1 Tomb of State of Chu in Jiangling, Hubei Province)

Fig. 24 Embroidery Design

5. Straight Unlined Garment

Among the examples of clothing and ornaments of the Warring States Period found in the Horse Brick No. 1 Tomb in Jiangling, Hubei Province, are around a dozen costumes of various kinds — clothes made of thin soft silk, silk gauze, brocade, gauze and silk ribbon. These are the earliest items ever discovered. Among them articles embroidered in gold and silver threads are the most numerous and the finest. The usual practice was to adopt the "lock" method of embroidery. In one example, scores of tigers, with fangs bared and showing their claws, are embroidered in scarlet, gold, silver grey and black, in irregular lines, on a piece of black silk gauze. As all the lines are embroidered on the obverse side, they are hardly detectable on the reverse side. Each unit of the pattern is rectangular in shape and measures 28.5 cm in length. On one part of the picture there are soaring phoenixes above a small curled-up dragon. On the other part, there is a scene of combat between a dragon and a tiger, the latter roaring in anger, the former coiling back in preparation for the attack. Their expressions couldn't be more lifelike; neither could the entire work be more naturalistic. The whole design is a masterpiece of dense stitches alternating with loose ones balanced in pleasing proportion, and of rhythmic composition. In short, both colour and pattern striking and the robe is a fine and rare work of art.

To make this kind of robe, the usual method was the "unity cut", i.e., material was folded in half and cut into the proper shape of the front and back pieces together with the two sleeves so that there are no seams to destroy the unity of the design. The width of either piece (front/back plus sleeve) was about the same as the width of the material itself. The characteristic feature of this kind of robe was a shawl collar having a straight extended band which was buttoned on the right. The body, sleeves and hems were even and straight, without evident curve; and decorative borders were added to collar and cuffs, and carried along the lapel and down the straight right hand opening of the robe. The borders around the cuffs were usually silk stripes of two colours.

6. Jacket and Trousers

In the middle of the Warring States Period, a national minority called Baidi established a dukedom in the central plains of China and named it the State of Zhongshan. The most popular costume for women of this national minority was a tight-fitting narrow-sleeved jacket called *ru*, which reached the waist and was usually matched with a check skirt.

Fig. 25 Two-piece costume comprising a narrow-sleeved short jacket and a check long skirt (Drawing of reconstructed costume of unearthed jade figurine)

Ancient Times 25

7. Spiral-shaped One-piece Garment

Compared with other costumes, apart from being a one-piece garment, the *shenyi* had another distinctive feature called *"xuren goubian"*. As *ren* refers to the lapel, *xuren* means an extended lapel, while *goubian* describes the style of the dress. Departing from the usual tailoring method of opening slits at the hems, the new approach was to sew up the front and the back pieces on the left hand side of the dress. Then the lapel of the back piece was extended so that the lengthened lapel formed a triangle. When worn, the lengthened piece was wound to the back and the garment was fastened by tying a girdle at the waist. Robes of this sort can now be clearly seen from the male and female figurines unearthed at Changsha County, Hunan Province, and Yunmeng County, Hubei Province. Such a pattern is also seen in a drawing on plain white silk found in a tomb of the State of Chu in Changsha. For example, a picture unearthed at this tomb shows the male occupant of the tomb in a high hat and large-sleeved robe, with the lapel winding down — a typical pattern of *shenyi*. Another picture shows a woman, her hair tied into a bun at the back of her head, wearing a tight-fitting loose-sleeved gown, trailing on the floor. On the gown are wavy patterns.

This was also a form of spiral-shaped one-piece garment. These dresses were usually made of soft thin materials and bordered with thick gold and silver threads at the extreme edges so as to reveal the silhouette of the dress. The more distinguished garments had the sleeves ornamented with silk or gold threads of light or dark texture, which produced a highly ornamental effect.

Fig. 26 Spiral-shaped robe (From a reconstructed drawing on silk)

Fig. 27 Robed female in the State of Chu (Drawing on silk from a tomb of Chu State at Chen Family Mountain, Changsha, Hunan Province)

26 Ancient Times

28

29

30

Fig. 31 Male figures of the Warring States Period wearing spiral-shaped one-piece garment with wound lapel (Wooden figurines unearthed in Changsha, Hunan Province)

Fig. 28 A servant in *shenyi* with big sleeves and wound lapel (Bronze human figure holding a lamp. A grade-three artifact from Pingshan, Hebei Province)

Fig. 29 A nobleman in high hat and long robe (Drawing on silk unearthed from a tomb of Chu State at Zidanku, Changsha, Hunan Province)

Fig. 30 Spread of wound-lapel one-piece garment with big sleeves (Drawing based on reconstructed costume of bronze figure unearthed at Pingshan, Hebei Province)

31   32

Ancient Times 27

33

Fig. 32 A nobleman dressed in spiral-shaped garment with wound lapel and colour embroidery (Colour drawing of wooden figurine. An article of antiquity, the original of which is now owned by Leiden Museum (Holland) and Metropolitan Fine Art Gallery (USA))

Fig. 33 Women's spiral-shaped costume with narrow sleeves (Drawing based on the design of a reconstructed bronze kettle unearthed in Chengdu, Sichuan Province)

Fig. 34 Women in spiral-shaped one-piece garments with narrow sleeves (Designs on bronze kettle unearthed in Chengdu, Sichuan Province)

34

8. Armour and *Hu Fu*

Ancient armour for warriors was mostly made of the skin of rhinoceroses or sharks and decorated with colourful drawings. During the Shang and Zhou Dynasties, in addition to leather armour, there was also armour made from silk and iron. Of the latter two the silk armour appeared earlier and was mostly made of plain silk thickly lined with cotton; it therefore had a protective function. Iron armour first appeared in the middle of the Warring States Period, and was preceded by bronze armour, a comparatively simple breast plate in the shape of a beast's face. From hitherto unearthed relics it can be inferred that bronze armour of the Western Zhou Dynasty had tiny holes probably for patching leather on it so that it could be used in conjunction with leather (or cloth) armour. The iron armour of the Warring States Period was usually made of iron strips strung together in the form of fish scales or willow leaves.

The *dou wu* (helmet), also called *zhou, shou kai, tou wu* or *kui,* was of different types, some round and pieced together from very small iron strips, others made of bronze cast into the shape of animals' faces. At the top of such bronze helmets there was often a bronze tube in which the tail of an ancient bird of prey, or a bird's feather, or a tassel could be fixed, as ornament. The surface of the helmets was mostly ground smooth, while the inside was course, rough and uneven. From this it can be surmised that a warrior wearing a helmet of this kind invariably had a turban on his head.

The ancient bronze mirror unearthed at the town of Shanbiao in Ji County, Henan Province reflects the characteristics of ancient military uniforms. On this bronze mirror 290 figures are carved, some in small round visored caps, others wearing a *dou wu* ornamented with sharp-angled objects. The clothes they wear are typical of *hu fu* — close-fitting and mostly just reaching the knees.

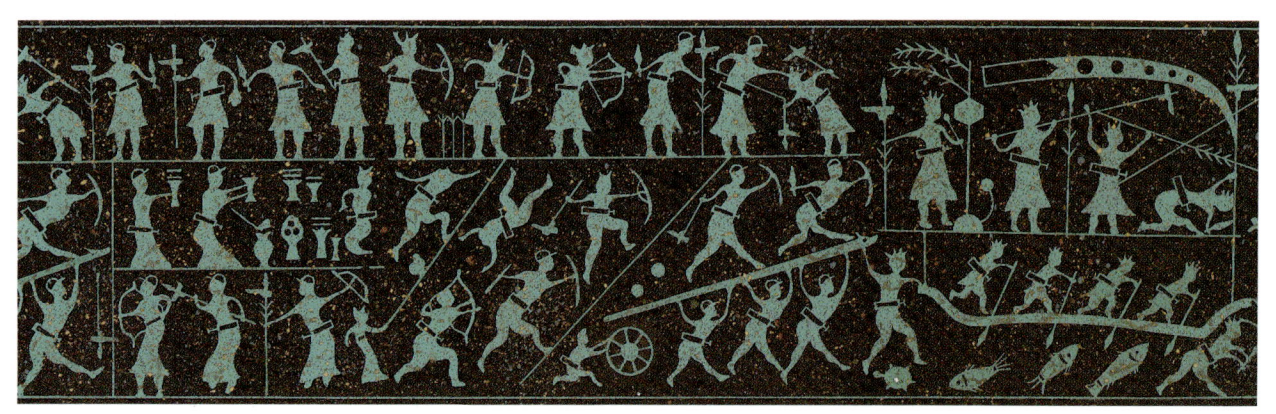

Fig. 35　Bronze *dou wu* of the Warring States Period (From excavations in Liaoning Province)

Fig. 36　Iron *dou wu* of the Warring States Period (From excavations in Yi County, Hebei Province)

Fig. 37　Warriors' outfit in the Warring States Period (Drawing based on designs of the bronze mirror unearthed at the town of Shanbiao, Ji County, Henan Province)

Fig. 38　Male figure in cap and narrow-sleeved gown reaching to the knees (Bronze figure of the Warring States Period from excavations at Shangcun Ridge, Sanmen Gorge, Henan Province)

Fig. 39　A servant wearing narrow-sleeved jacket (Sculpture of a lamp-holder unearthed in Mancheng, Hebei Province)

Fig. 40　Acrobat in narrow-sleeved jacket (Bronze figure of the Warring States Period in Frill Art Gallery, Washington DC, USA)

Fig. 41　A Warring States Period woman, double-braided and wearing 'hu fu' (Bronze figure from excavations at Gold Village, Luoyang, Henan Province)

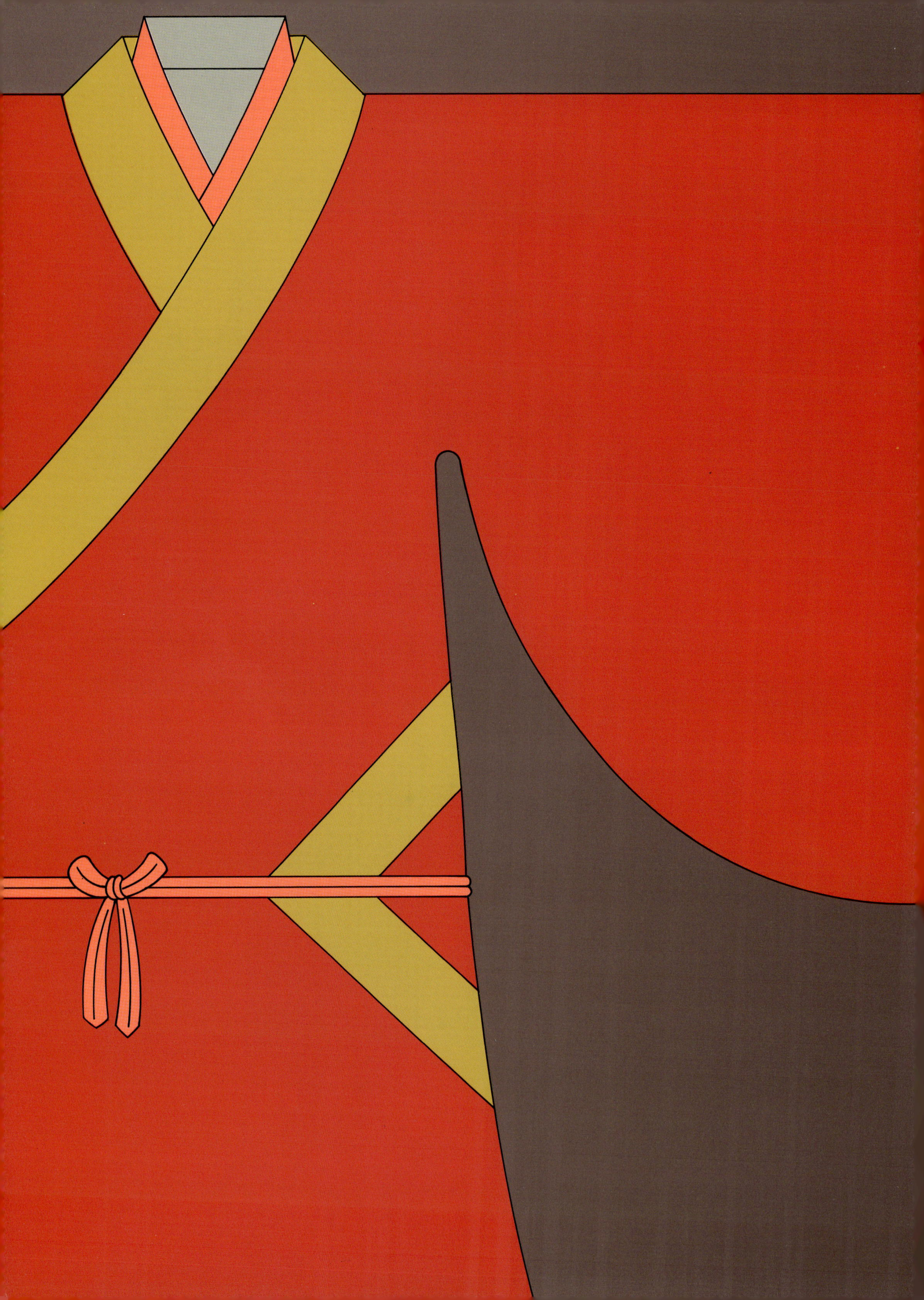

秦漢

QIN AND HAN DYNASTIES

Costume was one of the many institutions established after the Emperor of Qin unified China. When the Han Dynasty was founded after the collapse of Qin, it inherited what remained and the old institutions were, for the most part, intact. Han's economy and culture developed rapidly and China became strong and prosperous. During the reign of Emperor Wu, a high official named Zhang Qian was twice sent as an envoy to the Western Regions (Central Asia). His success in establishing communication between these regions and China proper promoted economic and cultural interchange between the Han people and the national minorities as well as between China and the neighbouring countries. As a consequence, Chinese costumes became more varied in design and richer in colour.

It was not until the second year of the reign of Emperor Xiaoming (A. D.59) that new costume regulations were devised for sacrificial rituals and official occasions. They elaborately prescribed the use of caps, dresses, boots and ribbons by people of different rank, thus firmly establishing the costume system of the Han Dynasty. But it was chiefly through the headgear that a person's social status was indicated. The most typical are *mian guan, chang guan, wu guan, fa guan* and *jin xian guan*. According to the rules, *mian guan* was to be worn along with the official costume only by emperors, princes, dukes and ministers on grand ritual occasions. *Chang guan* was created by the Han Emperor Liu Bang in his youth, so it was also called "Liu's Cap". Made of green bamboo bark, it was worn by civil officials when they offered sacrifices to the gods. *Wu guan* was worn by military officers at all levels on formal occasions. The imperial attendants and eunuchs also wore *wu guan*, adorned with marten's tails and gold ornaments. Judges wore *fa guan,* while scholars had *jin xian guan*, with the wearer's rank distinguished by the number of bars which ran across the top of the cap: three bars for aristocrats, two for officials down to the rank of court academician and one for those below. There were also several other kinds of caps for different occasions.

It was common in the Qin Dynasty (221-207 B.C.) to award army officers kerchiefs to be worn along with their caps. This custom was only practised in the army. Kerchiefs were in general use in Western Han (206 B.C. -A.D. 7). There were two kinds: one, pointed at the top, had the look of a gable-roof; the other was flat at the top. They were the essential head dress for men in the Han Dynasty. Petty functionaries, who were not permitted to wear caps, had to be content with kerchiefs. Officials who were entitled to the use of caps wore them on top of the kerchief. At home, however, it was permissible for them to wear kerchiefs without hats. There was also a definite code governing the wearing of the kerchief by people of different status, age and occupation.

Robes, mostly loose-sleeved, were the main type of men's clothing in the period of Qin and Han. Such robes were the official costume worn by officials when they were received in audience by the emperor or when they met each other on formal occasions. On ordinary occasions, however, they wore unlined garments somewhat resembling robes. All these clothes are divided into two types: "the spiral-shaped one-piece garment" and "the straight robe". The former had been the vogue during the period of the Warring States and remained popular in the early days of Han. However, during the East Han Dynasty it was replaced by the straight robe except on very formal occasions.

The official costume of Han was further characterized by the wearing of a silk ribbon. The aristocrats were accustomed to wearing not only swords but also a silk girdle and a silk ribbon attached to an official seal. Since the seal and the ribbon symbolized the power vested in an official, they were uniformly issued by the court. According to the system, officials carried their seal in a leather bag fastened on the waistband, with the silk ribbon hanging outside. Size, colour and texture of the silk ribbons worn by different persons, from the emperor down to officials at all levels, were so markedly distinguishable that one could tell at a glance the social status of the wearer. For example, as far as colour was concerned, there were reddish yellow ribbons for the emperor, red ones for princes, purple for the nobility or generals, and blue or black for officials below.

It was the vogue during the Han Dynasty for women to have their hair dressed in a bun and the shapes of the bun were varied and many: it might be tied at the top or at the back of the head, or it might be split in two and worn on both sides. The braiding of hair was done in the following manner: first part the hair in the middle, next braid the two strands of hair into one, and then create a variety of patterns by twisting the braid upwards. During the reign of Emperor Shun, a slanting bun was very popular. The hair could also be coiled up in all sorts of fashions and from it was always hung a tress of hair. It remained the main hairstyle down to the period of Wei and Jin. For head dressing, the aristocratic women wore *bu yao* — an ornament stuck to the hairpin which contained a miniature flower or animal and from which hung a string of coloured jewellery. This was still worn as an ornament in the Tang Dynasty (618-907). Besides '*bu yao*', some women also wore hairpins set with pearls or emeralds. But as a rule, women of low position did not wear *bu yao*. Instead they had their hair tied up with a turban or fixed with a few hairpins.

In the Han Dynasty, as of old, the one-piece garment remained the formal dress for women. However, it was somewhat different from that of the Warring States Period, in that it had an increased number of curves in the front and broadened lower hems. Close-fitting at the waist, it was always tied with a silk girdle.

Another kind of garment was called *gui yi,* and was similar to the former in appearance. Its front part spiralled to form at the lower end two ornamental pieces, broad at the top but narrow at the bottom, after the shape of a *daogui* (a Chinese measuring tool for herb medicine), hence the name *gui yi*. Women also wore jacket and skirt. The skirt was mostly sewn up with four pieces of white silk into a bell shape without decorative borders. At both ends of the waist part a silk band was sewn so that the skirt could be tied when worn. A pair of crotchless pants was worn underneath with each of the upper ends fastened to the thigh by a band. Later, crotched pants emerged in the imperial court.

In the Han Dynasty there were strict rules governing the proper use of shoes: official shoes went with ritual costumes; ordinary shoes went with court costumes; hempen sandals were for home wear and clogs for out-of-doors. During the nuptial ceremony a bride also wore painted clogs tied with multi-coloured silk ribbons.

In the Qin Dynasty, suits of armour were usually made from a whole piece of leather or thick silk fabric covered with pieces of metal or rhinoceros skin. After the Western Han Dynasty, however, steel armour came into general use and became the essential equipment of the army.

34 Qin and Han Dynasties

1. Emperor's *Mian Guan*, *Mian Fu* and *Chi Xi*

The *mian guan* was the official headgear worn by monarchs and officials of antiquity when they attended grand sacrificial rituals. It continued to be used as before by emperors, aristocrats and high-ranking officials in the Han Dynasty. On its top was a long board called a *'yan'* which was round in the front, flat at the back, about 7 inches in width and a foot in length. The upper end of the *'yan'* was usually hung with jewellery threaded on coloured strings. The quantity and quality of the jewellery used served as an important mark to distinguish the rank of the wearer. According to Han rules, for an emperor's cap there should be twelve strings of white jade; for princes or dukes, seven strings of blue jade; for ministers, five strings of black jade. The *mian guan* was for the most part black in colour with red and green lining inside. On either side of the cap there was a hole for an emerald hairpin to pass through and it was by this means that the cap was fastened to the bun of hair underneath. A silk cord was tied to one end of the hairpin. It passed under the chin and was then tied to the other end. On either side of the cap, somewhere about the ear, hung a pearl or a piece of jade called *chong er* (meaning "stuffing the ear"). Instead of stuffing the ear, however, they were only hung about the ears with the symbolic significance that the wearer should not believe any slander; this gave rise to the proverb "Stuffing the ear and refusing to listen.".

As a rule, the *mian guan* should be worn with the official costume. The official costume consists of a black garment and a red skirt embroidered with attractive designs. In addition, there should be a pair of breeches folded at the knee, a silk ribbon and a pair of shoes to form a complete ensemble. This kind of dress remained in use for over two thousand years — dating back to the Zhou Dynasty (1122-249 B.C.) and lasting through the Han, the Tang, the Song, and the Yuan, right up to the Ming Dynasty (1368-1644).

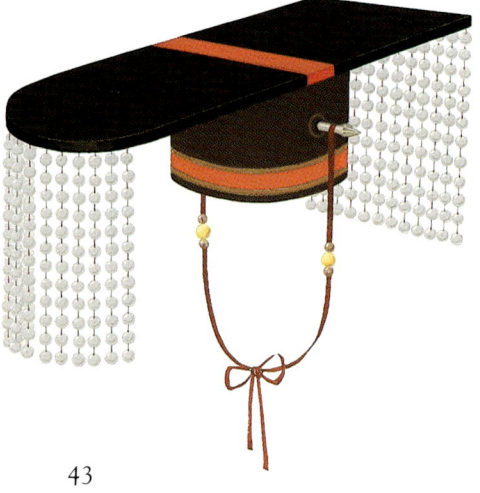

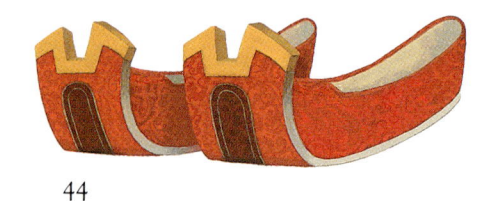

42

43

44

Qin and Han Dynasties 35

45

46

Fig. 42 Emperor's *mian fu* (Drawing based on historical documents and pottery figurines from Han Tombs at Jinan and Yinan, Shangdong Province)

Fig. 43 Emperor's *mian guan* (Same source as above)

Fig. 44 Emperor's *chi xi* (Same source as above)

Fig. 45 Officials in *mian guan* (Rubbing from stone relief unearthed at Yinan, Shangdong Province)

Fig. 46 Officials in *mian guan* (Coloured pottery figurines from excavations at Jinan, Shangdong Province)

2. Men's Robes

During the period of Qin and Han, the robe was considered the luxury wear for men. It was, as previously, worn on formal occasions. Its sleeves were loose, getting narrower toward the cuffs. Both the collar and the sleeves had decorative borders, while the collar was usually v-shaped, showing the garments beneath. Numerous men's robes depicted in the frescoes of a Han tomb unearthed in Wangdu, Hebei Province, were styled this way. In addition, the robes had low-cut collars with a large lapel tilted across the chest. The hem was usually densely pleated and some took the form of a crescent moon.

To match the robe, a court official was required to wear a kerchief and a *jin xian guan* on top of it. An example of this may be seen in the stone figures found in the excavation of a Han Tomb in Yinan, Shangdong Province. It can be seen from the figures that the official was dressed in such attire for a formal occasion. He also wore a white writing brush behind the ear. According to Han Dynasty custom, an official would use a brush to write memorials for the emperor at court sessions. After he had finished writing, he would pin the brush in his hair near his ear. With the passage of time, it became a rule that whenever civil officials were received in audience by the emperor, they had to wear a brush in this traditional manner. As this was now a mere decoration, the brush had no ink on the tip and was hence called a "white brush hairpin" in the records.

Fig. 47 Grey robe with lozenge patterns (Reconstructed painting based on frescoes in Han Tombs at Wangdu, Hebei Province and at Yinan, Shangdong Province, and on the actual pattern on an object unearthed from a Han Tomb at Mawangdui)

Fig. 48 A male-servant in gown and kerchief (Fresco in a Han Tomb excavated at Wangdu, Hebei Province)

Fig. 49 An official in *liang guan* and robe (Fresco in a Han Tomb excavated at Wangdu, Hebei Province)

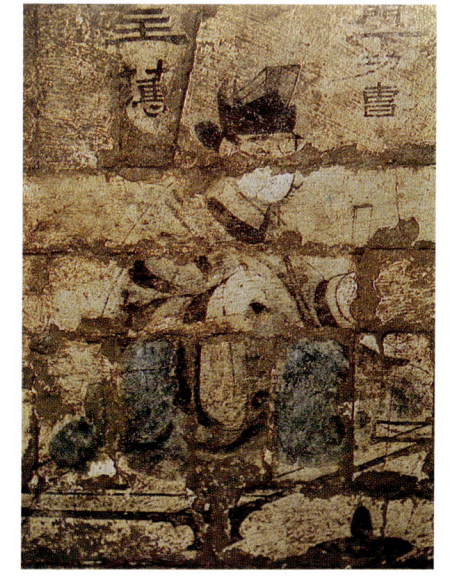

Fig. 50 An official in *liang guan* and robe (Coloured painting of Taocanglou building excavated at Hewang Village in Xingyang County, Henan Province)

Fig. 51 An official in *liang guan* and robe wearing brush hairpin (Rubbing from stone relief unearthed at Yinan, Shangdong Province)

Fig. 52 A civil official in *jin xian guan* and robe (Brick relief unearthed at Qinggangpo, Eastern Village, Chengdu, Sichuan Province)

38 Qin and Han Dynasties

3. Spiral-shape One-piece Garment

This was the vogue in the period of the Warring States (475-221 B.C.) and remained so in the early days of the Han Dynasty. This is evidenced by the fact that the wooden male images unearthed from a Han Tomb at Dafentou, Yunmeng County, Hubei Province and the painted figures of armed guards found on the hollow bricks unearthed in Luoyang are wearing such garments.

The spiralling type of garment was not only worn by men but was also a popular dress for women at the time. It was close-fitting, and reached to the ground with its lower part spreading out like a bell. Thus the feet are not shown even in walking. The sleeves, whose cuffs are often fringed, are either loose or tight. The collar is distinctive, with its lapels crossed and low enough to reveal the clothes beneath. As it was the custom then to show the collar of every piece of clothing, very often as many as three collars were seen round the neck, hence the name of "three-collar garment".

The garment shown in Fig. 59, known as a *gui yi,* was a style of dress popular with Han women. It is called *gui,* because its hanging part, broad at the top but narrow at the bottom, looks like a *dao gui* (ancient measuring tool for Chinese medicine). Garments of this kind are found on the Han Dynasty female ceramic figurines unearthed in Tongshan, Xuzhou, Jiangsu Province.

Fig. 53 Spiral-shaped one-piece garment (Drawing after restored pottery figurines unearthed in Xianyang, Shaanxi Province)

Fig. 54 Male figure in spiral-shaped one-piece garment (Pottery figurine of Han Dynasty unearthed in Xianyang, Shaanxi Province)

Fig. 55, 57 Male figures in hat and spiral-shaped one-piece garment (Pottery figurines of Han Dynasty unearthed in Xianyang, Shaanxi Province)

40 Qin and Han Dynasties

58

59

Fig. 58 Spiral-shaped one-piece garment (Drawing based on restored pottery figurines unearthed in such places as Xian and Xuzhou)

Fig. 59 A Woman in spiral-shaped one-piece garment (Pottery figurine in a Han Tomb unearthed at Tongshan, Xuzhou City, Jiangsu Province)

Qin and Han Dynasties 41

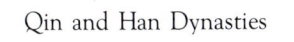

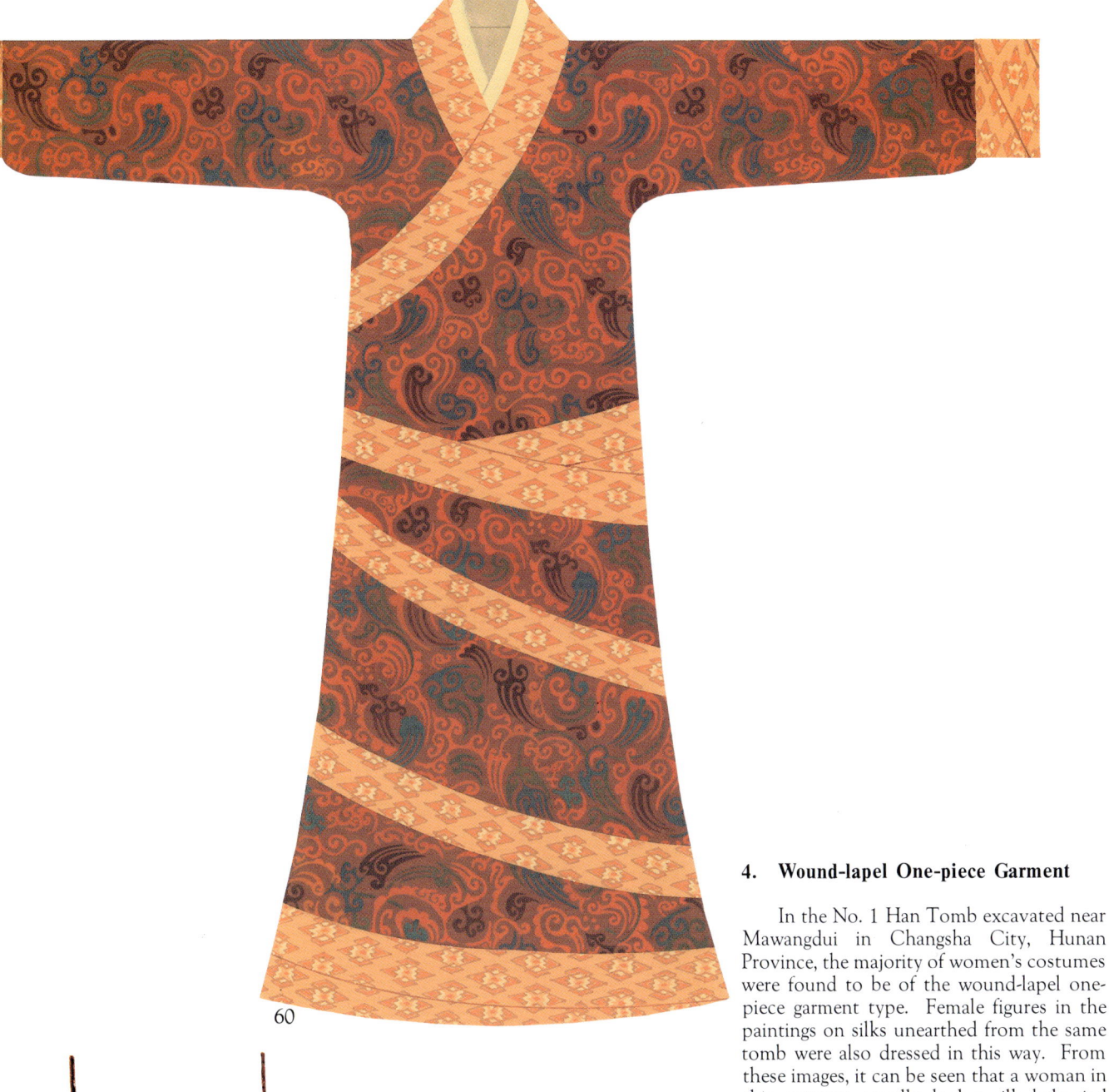

4. Wound-lapel One-piece Garment

In the No. 1 Han Tomb excavated near Mawangdui in Changsha City, Hunan Province, the majority of women's costumes were found to be of the wound-lapel one-piece garment type. Female figures in the paintings on silks unearthed from the same tomb were also dressed in this way. From these images, it can be seen that a woman in this garment usually had a silk belt tied closely round the waist or hips, so that it would not come loose. The belt position was decided by the length of the garment.

Fig. 60 Wound-lapel one-piece garment with narrow sleeves (Drawing based on restored wooden figurines found in No. 1 Han Tomb at Dafentou, Yunmeng County, Hubei Province)

Fig. 61 Servants in *chang guan* and wound-lapel one-piece garment with narrow sleeves (Wooden figurines from Han Tomb at Mawangdui in Changsha, Hunan Province)

42 Qin and Han Dynasties

62

63

Fig. 62 Wound-lapel one-piece garment with loose sleeves (Based on restored painting on silks from No. 1 Han Tomb at Mawangdui in Changsha, Hunan Province)

Fig. 63 A woman in wound-lapel one-piece garment with loose sleeves (Same source as above)

5. Women's Straight Robe

The straight robe was worn by both men and women. Though it appeared as early as the Western Han period, it had never been accepted as a ceremonial costume. The reason was that ancient pants were crotchless, with the two ends fastened to the waist with a band. The crotchless trousers had to be covered by a garment outside, as it was considered disrespectful to reveal one's trousers in those days. The spiral-shape one-piece garment was introduced for this purpose. Later, with steady improvement of costume, the shape of trousers was improved and the crotch evolved, making the spiral-shaped one-piece robe unnecessary. Beginning from the Eastern Han Dynasty, the straight robe became popular and gradually replaced the spiral-shaped one-piece garment.

Fig. 64 Women's straight robe (Drawing based on clothing found in No. 1 Han Tomb at Mawangdui in Changsha, Hunan Province)

Fig. 65 A woman in straight Robe (Coloured pottery figurine of Han Dynasty)

Fig. 66 Printed crimson silk straight robe (Based on real object from No. 1 Han Tomb at Mawangdui in Changsha, Hunan Province)

44 Qin and Han Dynasties

6. Women's Jacket and Skirt

Women began to wear the jacket and skirt as early as the Warring States Period. This dress system remained unchanged even in the Han Dynasty, when women donned jacket and skirt for ordinary wear. There is a line in a Han poem that reads: "The skirt tied with a band; the jacket joined by two enormous sleeves". Generally speaking, the jacket was short, reaching the waist only; while the skirt could be long enough to touch the ground. A jacket with a light-blue spun silk outer face ('shell' fabric) and silk floss for wadding was found in a Han Tomb at Mozuizi in Wuwei County, Gansu Province. The cuffs were joined by extra lengths of white silk. The skirt, too, was padded with silk floss.

The jacket and skirt system played a major role in Chinese women's costume. For a period of time after Eastern Han, its popularity declined, and it was not until the period of Wei and Jin that it became popular again. From that time onwards it was in vogue until the time of the Qing Dynasty — more than two thousand years all told. In spite of changes in length and size, the basic form and style of the jacket and skirt remained more or less the same as in earlier years.

Fig. 67 Women's jacket and skirt (Drawing from objects found in Han Tombs at Mozuizi in Wuwei County, Gansu Province and at Mawangdui in Changsha, Hunan Province)

Qin and Han Dynasties 45

7. Female Dancer's Costume

The periods of Qin and Han witnessed a considerable improvement in the artistic performances of dance and music. Professional singers, dancers and musicians appeared, and their pictures are seen in quite a number of the Han frescoes and stone and brick carvings. The picture here shows the ceramic figurine of a female dancer in Eastern Han, with her hair dressed in a large bun lavishly adorned with pearls and emeralds. She wears a full length robe that trails on the ground. The lapel is opened on the left, and the cuffs are extended into long and narrow false sleeves. This unique sleeve is the forerunner of the 'shui xiu' (a sleeve that flows like water waves), which is typical of traditional Chinese stage costumes.

Fig. 68 Dancing costume (Drawing based on reconstructed fresco and brick relief of Han Dynasty)

Fig. 69 A female dancer in dancing costume (From coloured painting of Taocanglou Building excavated at Hewang Village in Xingyang County, Henan Province)

46 Qin and Han Dynasties

Fig. 70 A female dancer in long-sleeved dancing costume (Pottery figurine from a Han Tomb in Guangzhou)

Fig. 71 Female dancers in long-sleeved dancing costume and wearing swallow-tail bun (Eastern Han brick relief from excavations in Peng County, Sichuan Province)

Fig. 72-73 Armour for commanding officers of Qin Dynasty (Drawing based on reconstructed Qin warrior figurines unearthed at Lintong, Shaanxi Province)

70

71

8. Armour

The pottery figurines of warriors from excavations in Lingtong County, Shaanxi Province, may be seen to be wearing seven different styles of armour, which can be classified into two main categories. One has a protective part made of leather, inlaid with scales of metal, rhinoceros skin or other materials. This armour, with a broad edge all around, was part of a commanding officer's uniform. The other type is made of square or rectangular shaped scales strung together, and was worn by ordinary soldiers. The armour was simply pulled over the head and then buckled up to fasten it. More often than not, a war-robe was worn underneath. The metal scales were mostly strung into plates that were either fixed or movable. The fixed plates were for the protection of chest and back, while the movable ones were for the shoulders, abdomen, waist and neck. Styles varied with arms and rank. For instance, infantrymen's armour was quite long, while that of cavalrymen was comparatively short. The armour for the rank and file was much simpler in design and contained larger scales as compared with that of imperial guards. The armour for a commanding officer was of an even more complicated structure, sometimes with exceptionally elaborate patterns.

Iron armour was popularized in the Western Han period and gradually became part of the standard uniform for the army. One may see model armour of this type from the figurines unearthed near Yangjiawan in Xianyang County, Shaanxi Province.

Though diverse in style, armour in this period was invariably painted black. Specifically, there were two kinds of armour. One was the rectangular *zha jia* (tied coats of mail), so called because the breast and back plates were tied upon the shoulder. Sometimes a cape was worn over the mail. This kind of armour was supposed to be for ordinary soldiers. The other kind consisted of smaller plates resembling fish scales, with the parts under the waistline and at the cape retaining the form of *zha jia* so that the wearer could conveniently lean forward or backward. This is thought to have been the military attire of commanding officers.

48 Qin and Han Dynasties

Fig. 74 Armour for officers and men of Qin Dynasty (Drawing based on reconstructed Qin warrior figurines unearthed at Lintong, Shaanxi Province)

Fig. 75 Armour for ordinary soldiers of Qin Dynasty (Same source as above)

Fig. 76-77 Armour for commanding officers of Han Dynasty (Drawing based on reconstructed pottery figurines unearthed at Yangjaiwan in Xianyang County, Shaanxi Province)

50 Qin and Han Dynasties

Fig. 78 Armour for ordinary soldiers of Han Dynasty (Drawing based on reconstructed pottery figurines unearthed at Yangjiawan in Xianyang County, Shaanxi Province)

Fig. 79-80 Armour for commanding officers of Han Dynasty (Same source as above)

Fig. 81-84 Officers and men of Qin Dynasty clad in armour (Pottery figurines unearthed at Lintong, Shaanxi Province)

Qin and Han Dynasties 51

81

82

83

84

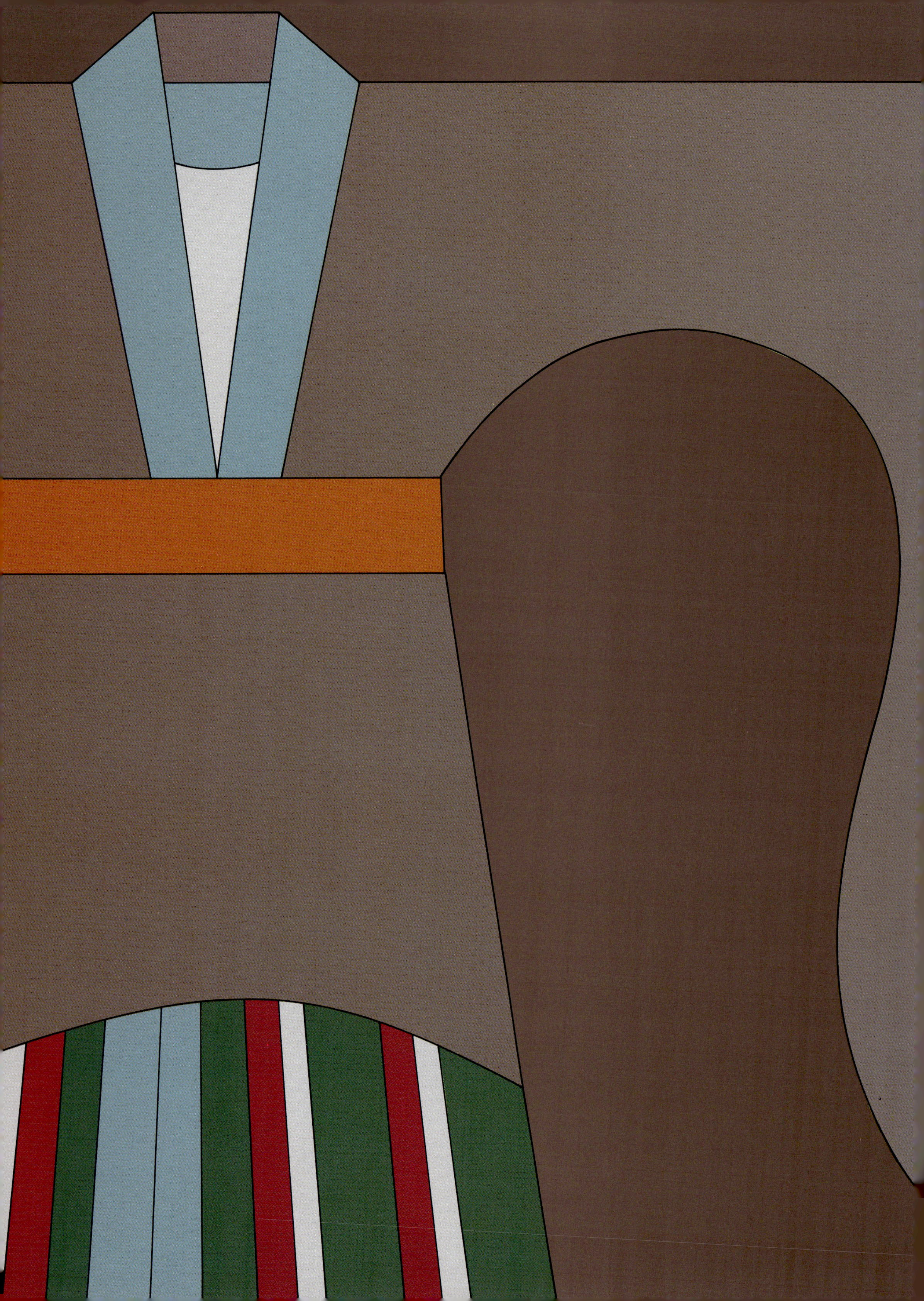

魏晋南北朝

WEI, JIN AND
THE SOUTHERN AND
NORTHERN DYNASTIES

During the period of the Wei, Jin and the Southern and Northern Dynasties, successive wars had a destabilising influence on the political and economic situation in various parts of the country. This affected every aspect of social life, including the systems of headgear and clothing, in which great changes took place.

On the whole, the costumes of the Wei and Jin period still followed the patterns of Qin and Han. During the Southern and Northern Dynasties, when some national minorities first established their own regimes, they still dressed according to their own customs and institutions. But later on, under the influence of Han culture, they began to wear the costume of the Hans. Emperors and their officials, in particular, indulged in the high hats and broad waist bands of the Han people. The most distinctive event in this period was the imposition of reforms by Emperor Xiao Wen of Northern Wei, historically known as "Emperor Xiao Wen's Reforms". As a result, all the officials of the Northern Dynasties wore the hats and costumes of the Han and Wei period. Due to the respect in which Han culture was held by the rulers of the national minorities, the traditional Han hats and costumes were retained even in the Ming Dynasty, and were invariably worn on important occasions such as sacrificial ceremonies and imperial court gatherings.

On the other hand, large numbers of northern people were compelled to leave their native place and migrate to the south due to the ever-increasing wars. As a result of this large-scale migration, millions of minority people began to settle in the central plains (the middle and lower reaches of the Yellow River) and live amongst the Han people. Consequently, the traditions and social customs of both Han and the minority people gradually intermingled. Many Han people started to wear *hu fu* (tartar costume), distinguished by its short jacket with narrow sleeves, waist-band and high leather boots. Women's costumes were also more or less influenced by those of the northern minority people. Generally, the original costumes characterized by their long upper part and short lower part were converted into a plain upper part and colourful lower part. In addition, the loose dress with a band also gave way to a tight-fitting garment. From then on, the fashion of cumbersome dress gradually disappeared, and was replaced by light and functional costumes. Before long, *hu fu* became the most popular fashion in the central plains area.

The main style of headdress in the Wei, Jin, and Southern and Northern Dynasties was a piece of silk cloth. According to historical records, towards the end of the Han Dynasty, some noblemen and celebrities refused to observe the court rites. They covered their heads with a piece of silk cloth as a mark of elegance, and this practice continued into the Wei and Jin period. Typical and detailed descriptions of this style can be seen in such paintings as "Seven Convivial Worthies in the Bamboo Grove", "Courtesans of Northern Qi", and "Eminent Scholars and Hermits".

Official headgear in this period also had special characteristics. Popular as the Han Dynasty's turban still was, it had nevertheless undergone several changes. For example, the turban was raised in the rear part and levelled in the middle, so that it became narrower towards the top, and was therefore commonly called the "levelled turban" or the "small hat". This kind of headgear was widely accepted by different ranks of people both north and south. When a cage-like cover was added to the top of the turban, it was called the "cage hat". This constituted the chief headdress for both men and women during the Wei, Jin and the Northern and Southern Dynasties. The hat was also called the "lacquered gauze cage hat", since the turban was made of black lacquered gauze. In addition, there were various other hats such as the "rolled lotus hat", the "peaked riding hat" and the "white high hat", most of which came from the north.

During this period, the main costume for Han men was the gown, which was of two kinds: the unlined and the lined. The gown differed from the robe of the Qin and Han period in that it was free from the restrictions of the past sleeve pattern and was quite loose at the cuffs. Especially in the Wei, Jin and the Southern Dynasties, everyone, from nobles and celebrities down to the common people, valued the loose gown with big sleeves. Influenced by the popularity of metaphysics, Buddhism and Taoism in the Wei and Jin period, some scholars broke with the old feudal rules by wearing loose costumes and even baring their necks and chests. Ji Kang, Liu Ling and others of the famous seven convivial worthies, for instance, wore loose robes with the collars wide open to bare their necks and chests. This reflects the typical features of costumes worn by scholars and celebrities in this period.

The principal costumes for men of national minorities in the north were the *ku zhe* (pleated coat and breeches) and the *liang dang* (waistcoat). Although the name *ku zhe* originated in late Han Dynasty, the basic costume pattern had long been in existence, and was a type of *hu fu* that used to be very popular in the Warring States Period. Through long years of reform and improvement, *ku zhe* became gradually more sophisticated. Between late and early Wei, the costume was chiefly worn by men in the army, but during Wei and Jin it was popularized among the general public and became a casual form of dress, though commanding officers and soldiers still kept it as their military uniform. The main feature of *ku zhe* was that the *zhe,* or coat, was small and tight fitting, and reached to the knees while the *ku,* or breeches, were loose, reaching to the feet. To make this kind of costume, various kinds of materials could be used, such as fine silk with colourful embroidered patterns, brocade or even animal furs. Those who wore *ku zhe* would use three-foot brocade ribbons to tightly fasten the knee part of the trouser legs for freedom of movement. That is why *ku zhe* was also called *fu ku* (fastened breeches). Leather belts were commonly used as waistbands for *fu ku,* those inlaid with gold and silver being considered the best. *Liang dang,* made of cotton or silk and tied with a leather belt round the waist, consisted of one chest piece and one back piece, which were connected on the shoulders with several leather loops. This fashion remained very popular even in the Tang and Song Dynasties.

Hairstyles for Han women during this period also had certain characteristics. The 'covered bun', a switch bun decorated with gold and jewellery, was for a time very much in fashion among aristocratic women.

Ordinary women, however, preferred to coil up their hair into other styles, though there were some who also wore the switch bun. In most cases the switch bun was tall and sometimes too tall to stand in its upright position, so that it fell over the temples and the eyebrows. There were also a considerable number of women who followed the customs of the national minorities in the western region and coiled up their hair in single or double loops so that it towered on top of the head. Then there were others who wore their hair in the shape of a fork or a spiral. In the Southern Dynasties, women influenced by Buddhism usually parted their hair in the middle at the top of their head to form a vertical bun, which was called the 'bun of the Flying Devils'. First appearing in the imperial court and then later popular among the ordinary people, this hairstyle can still be seen in many ancient Chinese paintings.

Han women's costumes were comprised of gown, trousers, jacket and skirt, all of which at first followed the official systems of Qin and Han but later on underwent constant changes. Most of the gowns were buttoned down the front, and the collar and cuffs were fringed with decorative borders. As for the skirts, they were usually worn with silk ribbons fastening the waist of the wearer. The northern minority women also wore waistcoats and breeches together with pleated coats. Though waistcoats were mostly for men, women were also allowed to wear them, at first only inside, but later outside a cross-collar coat or jacket. This kind of costume is mentioned in the Jin Dynasty novel "Ghost Hunt", which tells about the killing of a ghost by Zhong Yao, a minister in the Wei Dynasty. According to the tale, many people had had frequent encounters with ghosts in the area of Yingchuan Prefecture (now Xuchang City). One night, Zhong Yao was out on business when he saw a female ghost in the semblance of a woman in a white silk gown and red embroidered waistcoat. Quickly, Zhong Yao drew his sword and killed her, but the ghost staunched the blood with silk floss and fled. The following day, Zhong Yao sent his men to trace the bloodstains, and finally they found the body, which appeared as it had been on the previous night, with the difference that some silk floss had been taken from the waistcoat to staunch the blood. The story itself is, of course, a fantasy, but it shows that during this period, women did wear waistcoats outside their silk gowns. The waistcoat was delicately made, embroidered with colourful patterns and padded with silk floss. It was the origin of the present-day cotton-padded vest.

In addition, the northern women were also allowed to wear *ku zhe,* in conjunction with a cage hat and a waistcoat. In fact, this kind of women's outfit was very similar to men's attire of this period.

The shoes for both men and women were more or less the same as those of the previous dynasty, but the materials were much finer. There were different kinds of shoes, such as "silk shoes", "brocade shoes", and "leather shoes". Some, that were only worn by noblewomen, were called "fragrant dust shoes". Certain rules were set for the colours of the shoes: green, blue and white were for soldiers and labourers: red and blue were for maidservants and attendants. In addition, there were two kinds of wooden sandals: one had two spikes attached to the sole, one in front and the other at the heel; the other kind had two movable spikes which could be adjusted if necessary, and was suitable for climbing mountains. Shoes, however, were compulsory on important occasions, when anyone who wore wooden sandals would be regarded as disrespectful.

As warfare became more sophisticated, remarkable improvements were made in warriors' helmets and armour. The typical forms in this period were the tube-sleeve armour, the vest armour and the polished armour.

56 Wei, Jin and the Southern and Northern Dynasties

1. Lacquered Gauze Cage Hat and Loose Gown with Large Sleeves

Gu Kaizhi's painting "Fu to Luo River Goddess" was based on the *fu* — a descriptive poem in prose and verse — by Cao Zhi. In this vertical scroll, the image of the Luo River goddess is carefully depicted. Both her costume and headdress are in the fashion of the Eastern Jin. The men in the picture wear loose gowns with large flowing sleeves, a popular style among men of different social strata even in the Southern Dynasties period. The men's hats are also rather special: some wear small hats or wrap their heads with turbans; others are dressed in lacquered gauze cage hats.

The lacquered gauze cage hat was level at the top with two ear-flaps hanging down, and was one of the main headdresses in the Wei, Jin and the Southern and Northern Dynasties. Usually it was worn outside a turban, with silk ribbons to be tied up under the chin. This kind of hat originated in the Han Dynasty, but was originally roundish at the top and so slightly different from that of the Wei and Jin.

Fig. 85 Loose gown with large sleeves (Drawing based on frescoes and scrolls of Wei and Jin period)

Fig. 86 Lacquered gauze cage hat (Drawing based on paintings on plain white silk, frescoes and unearthed pottery figurines)

Wei, Jin and the Southern and Northern Dynasties 57

Fig. 87 A monarch in a water-chestnut-shaped kerchief and large-sleeved gown ("Monarchs of Various Dynasties" painted by Yan Liben)

Fig. 88 Aristocrats in loose gowns with large sleeves escorted by their attendants (Part of "Fu to Luo River Goddess" painted by Gu Kaizhi)

Fig. 89 A nobleman in curled beam hat and robe (Part of "Heroines in History", painting by Gu Kaizhi)

Fig. 90 An aristocrat in curled beam hat and large-sleeved gown. His attendant in cage hat and gown (Part of "Fu to Luo River Goddess", painting by Gu Kaizhi)

Fig. 91 A nobleman in cage hat and large-sleeved gown (Korean fresco)

Fig. 92-93 Scholars in small hat or kerchief and loose gown (Part of "Eminent Hermetic Scholars", painting by Sun Wei)

Fig. 94 Scholars in kerchiefs with gowns draped over their shoulders (Part of Northern Qi painting, "Courtesans")

Fig. 95 A scholar in kerchief and loose gown (Brick relief fresco of the Southern Dynasties unearthed at Xishan Bridge in Nanjing, Jiangsu Province)

Fig. 96 *Ku zhe* (Restoration based on unearthed pottery figurines)

Fig. 97 A man in *ku zhe* (Pottery figurine of the Northern Dynasties)

Wei, Jin and the Southern and Northern Dynasties 61

96

97

2. Ku Zhe

The *ku zhe* was a suit of clothes consisting of two parts. *Fu ku* (bound breeches) varied little and it was not until the period between late Northern Dynasties and Sui that a new pattern — the pleated bound breeches — emerged. The *zhe yi* (pleated coat), however, had many different styles. The sleeves, for example, could be wide or narrow, long or short. As for the front of the garment, it might be buttoned on the right, or more popularly down the front. Some people even tailored the hem of the front diagonally to form a small swallow-tail as the two front pieces covered each other.

62   Wei, Jin and the Southern and Northern Dynasties

98

3. Women's Multi-lap Swallowtail Costume

During the Wei, Jin and the Southern and Northern Dynasties, though men no longer wore the traditional one-piece garment, some women continued to do so. However, the style was quite different from that seen in the Han Dynasty. Typically, the women's dress was decorated with *xian* and *shao*. The latter refers to pieces of silk cloth sewn onto the lower hem of the dress, which were wide at the top and narrow at the bottom, so that triangles were formed overlapping each other. *Xian* refers to some relatively long ribbons which extended from the short-cut skirt. While the wearer was walking, these lengthy ribbons made the sharp corners on the lower hem wave like a flying swallow, hence the Chinese phrase "beautiful ribbons and flying swallowtail".

During the Southern and Northern Dynasties, costumes underwent further changes in style. The long flying ribbons were no longer seen and the swallowtailed corners became enlarged. As a result, the flying ribbons and swallowtailed corners were combined into one. This change may be seen in Gu Kaizhe's paintings "Heroines in History" and "*Fu* to Luo River Goddess", in lacquered paintings unearthed from Jinlong in Datong, Shaanxi Province, and in frescoes unearthed from a Korean tomb.

99

Fig. 98 Women's multi-lap swallowtail costume (Reconstructions based on silk paintings and frescoes)

Fig. 99 A woman in multi-lap swallowtail costume (Part of "Heroines in History" by Gu Kaizhi)

Fig. 100-101 Women in multi-lap swallowtail costumes (Part of "*Fu* to Luo River Goddess" by Gu Kaizhi)

Fig. 102 Women's multi-lap swallowtail costume (Reconstruction based on costumes from lacquer figure painting on screen unearthed in Datong, Shaanxi Province)
Fig. 103 Women in multi-lap swallowtail costume (Korean fresco)

Fig. 104 Women in multi-lap swallowtail costume (Screen in Northern Wei lacquer painting unearthed from tomb of Sima Jinlong in Datong, Shaanxi Province)

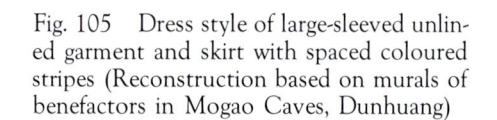

Fig. 105 Dress style of large-sleeved unlined garment and skirt with spaced coloured stripes (Reconstruction based on murals of benefactors in Mogao Caves, Dunhuang)

105

Fig. 106 An aristocratic woman in large-sleeved unlined garment and skirt with spaced coloured stripes, accompanied by her attendants (Mural in Mogao Cave 228, Dunhuang)

106

4. Women's Unlined Upper Garment and Skirt

On both sides of the corridors in the Mogao Caves in Dunhuang, or under the murals depicting Buddhist stories inside the caves, there are neat rows of figures ranging in size from a few inches to several feet. Among these figures can be seen important officials as well as common people. People had their images recorded on the walls to show they had donated funds for the work on the caves and had made offerings to the Buddha images inside. Hence they were called the masters and benefactors of the caves. Beside each figure was an inscription giving the name, seniority, post and rank of the donor, as well as the year in which the donation was made. These figures are a valuable source not only for the study of the evolution of Chinese costumes in various dynasties but also for research into the social life of ancient times.

From the costumes worn by the benefactors in the Dunhuang murals and the costumes of the pottery figurines unearthed in Luoyang, it can be seen that women's costumes in the period of Wei and Jin were generally large and loose. The upper garment opened at the front and was tied at the waist. The sleeves were broad and fringed at the cuffs with decorative borders of a different colour. The skirt had spaced coloured stripes and was tied with a white silk band at the waist. There was also an apron between the upper garment and skirt for the purpose of fastening the waist. Apart from wearing a multi-coloured skirt, women also wore other kinds such as the crimson gauze-covered skirt, the red-blue striped gauze double skirt, and the barrel-shaped red gauze skirt. Many of these styles are mentioned in historical records.

66 Wei, Jin and the Southern and Northern Dynasties

107

108

Fig. 107 Dress style of broad-sleeved upper garment with front opening and long skirt (Reconstruction based on unearthed pottery figurines)

Fig. 108 A woman in unlined upper garment with front opening and long skirt (Pottery figurine of the Northern Dynasties)

Fig. 109 Woman in unlined upper garment and skirt (Part of "Admonished Bluestockings", painting by Gu Kaizhi)

68 Wei, Jin and the Southern and Northern Dynasties

5. Costumes and Adornments of the Common People

A group of tombs dating back to the Wei and Jin period has recently been discovered in the Gobi Desert to the northeast of Jiayu Pass, Gansu Province. Six of those tombs have colour paintings on their brick walls. Numbering more than six hundred, all these brick paintings offer vivid pictures of the everyday life of the period including picking of mulberry leaves, farming, raising livestock, cultivating wasteland, cooking and feasting. Those depicting labourers alone number over two hundred, and give a valuable record of the life of the common people. In the paintings, the farmer's robe, the hunter's felt hat, the messenger's silk turban, the herdsman's puttee and the woman's skirt are depicted very realistically, presenting a unique record of costume types.

Fig. 110 A messenger in turban and robe (Brick painting unearthed at Jiayu Pass, Gansu Province)

Fig. 111 A woman in robe and apron picking mulberry leaves (Brick painting unearthed at Jiayu Pass, Gansu Province)

Fig. 112 A farmer and his wife wearing robes (Brick painting unearthed at Jiayu Pass, Gansu Province)

Fig. 113 A hunter in felt hat and robe (Brick painting unearthed at Jiayu Pass, Gansu Province)

114

115

116 117

Fig. 114 Musicians in small hats, short jackets and skirts (Pottery figurines of the Northern Dynasties)

Fig. 115 A man in a garment with front opening, narrow sleeves and low-cut v-neck (Colour pottery figurine of the Northern Dynasties, now in the Royal Canadian Museum)

Fig. 116 A woman in hat and wearing jacket and skirt (Pottery figurine of the Southern Dynasties, now in the National Museum of Kyoto, Japan)

Fig. 117 A servant in cage hat and wearing jacket and skirt (Pottery figurine of the Northern Dynasties)

70 Wei, Jin and the Southern and Northern Dynasties

6. Helmet and Armour

In the period of the Wei, Jin and the Southern and Northern Dynasties, there were three main kinds of armour.

The *tong xiu kai,* or tube-sleeve coat of mail, which developed from the armour of the Eastern Han Dynasties, was popular in the period of the Eastern and Western Jin. This kind of armour was made by stringing together numerous small protective pieces shaped like fish scales or tortoise shells, in the form of a tube. The front and back pieces were joined at the sides. Two tube-sleeves were attached to the shoulder for protection. In addition, the wearer wore a helmet with ear protectors. On the top of the helmet there was a tassel.

The *liang dang kai,* or vest armour, which resembles the waistcoat of the period was the main outfit of troops in the period of the Southern and Northern Dynasties. The materials used for making this vest armour were often hard metal or leather. Protective pieces were of two kinds: long striped pieces and scale-shaped pieces. The latter were always used for the front part of the armour, thus making it possible for the wearers to move easily during combat. In addition, warriors often wore a thick waistcoat inside as protection against chafing. They also wore helmets and, with very few exceptions, they wore pleated coats as well.

Ming guang kai, or shining armour, served to protect the chest and the back. It was usually made of iron or copper and was so polished that it shone like a mirror. When worn by combatants on the battlefield, the armour would give out dazzling light due to the irradiation of sunlight, hence the name "shining armour". It was characterized by its many styles: some were simple, others complicated; some provided only two round plates for chest and back, others were reinforced with shoulder and knee guards, while the more complicated ones had multiple shoulder plate protectors. In general, the body of the armour reached the buttocks and was fastened with a leather belt round the waist.

118

119

Wei, Jin and the Southern and Northern Dynasties

120

121

Fig. 118 A warrior in helmet and tube-sleeve armour (Extant pottery figurine)

Fig. 119 A warrior in helmet and tube-sleeve armour (Colour pottery figurine of the Northern Dynasties, now in Seinusky Art Gallery in France)

Fig. 120 Dress style of the vest armour (Reconstruction based on unearthed brick carvings, pottery figurines and frescoes)

Fig. 121 Warriors in helmets and vest armour (Mural in Mogao Cave 285, Dunhuang, Gansu Province)

72 Wei, Jin and the Southern and Northern Dynasties

Fig. 122 Dress style of the "shining armour" (Reconstruction based on unearthed pottery figurines and stone carvings)

Fig. 123 Brocade with pattern of incarnation of the celestial ruler (Relic unearthed at Asitana, Turfan, Xinjiang Uygur Autonomous Region)

122

Fig. 124 Embroidered portrait of Buddha (Relic unearthed at Mogao Caves in Dunhuang, Gansu Province)

Fig. 125 Brocade with pattern of the one-legged dragon-like monster (Relic unearthed at Asitana, Turfan, Xinjiang Uygur Autonomous Region)

Fig. 126 Embroidered decorative border (Relic unearthed at Mogao Caves in Dunhuang, Gansu Province)

Fig. 127 Brocade with patterns of animals within square frames (Relic unearthed at Asitana, Turfan, Xinjiang Autonomous Region)

Wei, Jin and the Southern and Northern Dynasties 73

123

127

124

125    126

7. Fabrics

The technology of textiles, embroidery and dyeing in this period developed rapidly, though hampered by frequent wars. All of the states paid much attention to the development of textiles, and as the Kingdom of Shu (based in present-day Sichuan) made the greatest effort in this respect, the production of Shu brocade expanded fast, and the product won a widespread renown.

According to historical records, a wide variety of brocades were produced during this period. Among these were the cave, the Miao (from a national minority), the velvet, and the Wuhou brocade, honouring the title of the Shu prime minister Zhu Geliang. In the novel "Ye — the Capital City", over a hundred kinds of brocade are mentioned, and even the difference in their texture, patterns and colour are described. With the increasing number of ancient relics now being discovered, a great many fabrics mentioned in the novel have been identified.

Judging from the abundant data now available, the chief patterns on these fabrics were the *xie* (a one-legged dragon-like monster from ancient fables), trees, animals within square frames and pairs of birds in linked rings. In addition, a number of patterns popular in Central and West Asia have been discovered. Among these are the incarnation of the celestial ruler, lotus flowers, and birds and animals linked with strings of pearls. The designs on these fabrics foreshadow the use of such later Sui and Tang brocade designs as pairs of animals linked with strings of pearls, and even inlaid jewels.

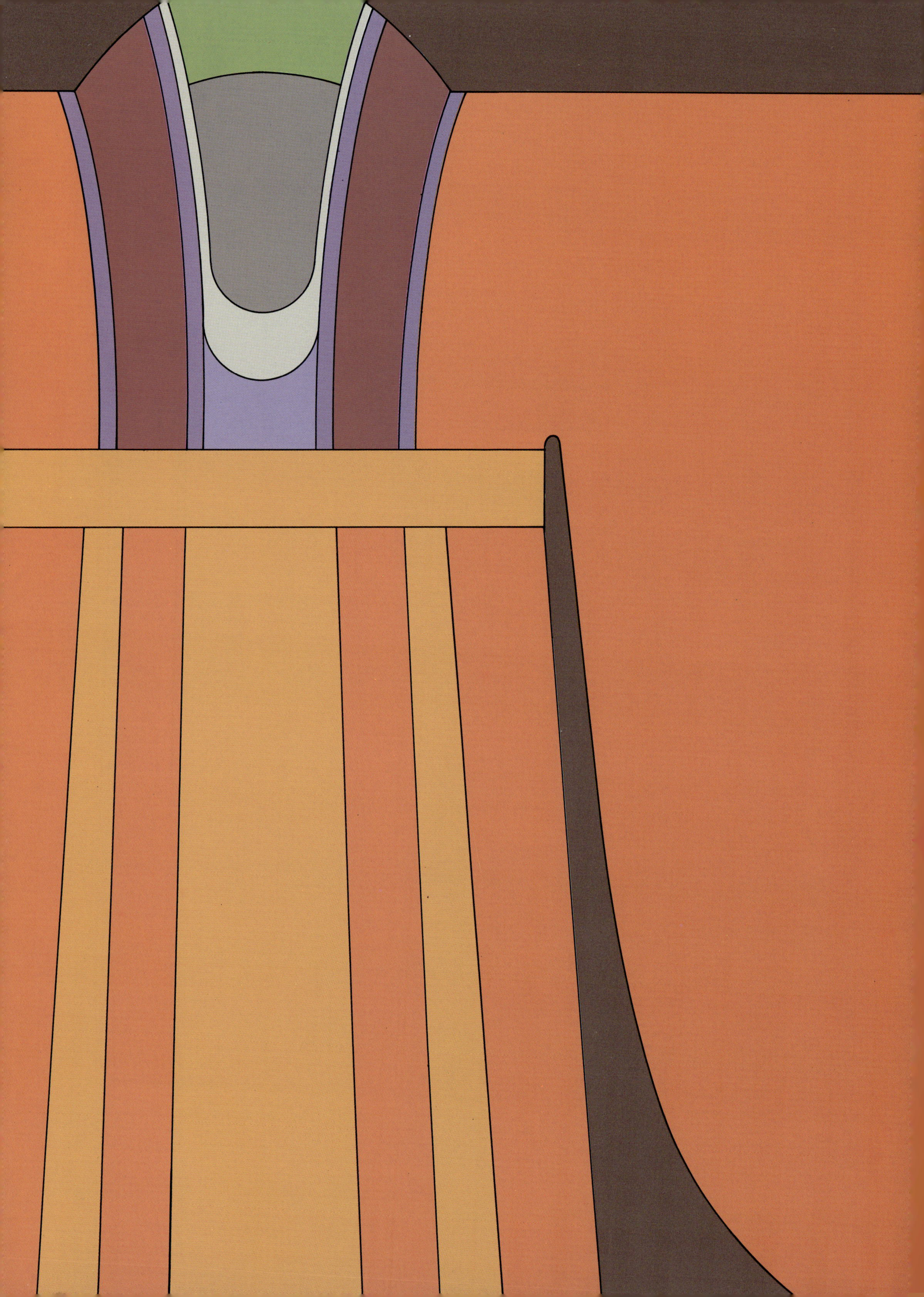

隋唐五代

SUI, TANG AND
THE FIVE DYNASTIES

78 Sui, Tang and the Five Dynasties

128

1. Emperor's Costumes and Accessories

Yan Liben, an outstanding painter of the Tang Dynasty, used to draw portraits for Emperor Taizong, and he was also directly involved in formulating the system of the Tang's costumes and accessories. Therefore, the costumes and accessories of monarchs that he drew can be taken as representative of the prevailing style. The costumes of the Tang Dynasty can be seen in Yan Liben's portraits and in the mural "The Emperor on a Journey" in Mogao Cave 220 in Dunhuang. Both the structure of the crowns together with the way of wearing the sword with ribbons attached and the arrangement of the dress ornaments are elaborately shown, thus providing evidence of the specific forms of official costume in that historical period.

Fig. 128 An emperor in crown and official costume accompanied by his attendants (Mural in Mogao Cave 220, Dunhuang)

Fig. 129 An emperor in crown and official costume with his attendants in caged hats and ceremonial clothes ("Portraits of Emperors of Various Dynasties" by Yan Liben)

129

Sui, Tang and the Five Dynasties 79

Fig. 130 Large-sleeved ceremonial dress
(Reconstruction based on unearthed pottery
figurines and frescoes)

2. Civil Officials' Ceremonial Dresses

Apart from the tight-sleeved robe with round collar, ceremonial dress was still worn by Tang officials on such important occasions as sacrificial ceremonies. The styles of such dress were largely based on the Sui system; they included turbans or cage hats for headgear, a large-sleeved gown with front opening and an apron over it, and a tasseled jade pendant attached to a girdle to complete the outfit.

131

132

133

Fig. 131, 133 Early Tang civil officials in turbans and large-sleeved gowns (Coloured pottery figurines. Originals now in Shanghai Museum)

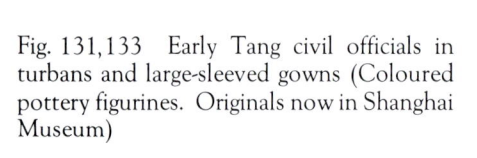

Fig. 132 Civil officials in lacquered gauze cage hats and large-sleeved ceremonial dresses (Frescoes in Li Xian's tomb, Qian Country, Shaanxi Province)

Sui, Tang and the Five Dynasties 81

3. *Fu Tou* and Robes

In the Tang Dynasty, *fu tou* (turban) and robes were the correct dress for men, as can be seen in the painting "Imperial Carriage" by Yan Liben. All of the men in the painting, except the Turbo envoys, wear *fu tou* and robes.

The *fu tou* was a kind of headdress developed after the kerchief of the Han and Wei Dynasties. From the Wei and Jin onward it became even more popular. During the reign of Emperor Wu of Northern Zhou, the kerchief was, for the sake of beauty and comfort, purposely tailored in such a way as to form four ribbon-shaped corners that kept the hair in place. With the coming of the Tang Dynasty, people added to the *fu tou* a fixed ornament called *jin zi* (decorative turban), whose shapes varied in different periods of the dynasty. In early Tang it was relatively low and its top was flat; then it was made higher and higher so that its central part became slightly concave and it looked like two separate halves. From mid Tang onwards the height of the decorative turban continued to increase, and, as a result, its top appeared like two balls. These are clearly shown in the frescoes and pottery figurines found in the tombs of Princes Zhang Huai and Yi De in Xian. The two corners (otherwise known as the "two feet"), also underwent many changes, and by late Tang and the beginning of the Five Dynasties, the original soft corners had been replaced by two stiff wings, one on each side.

In the fourth year of Zhen Guan (A.D. 630), rules were made to regulate the colours of robes worn by officials: purple for the third and fourth rank; bright red for the fifth; green for the sixth and seventh; and blue for the eighth and ninth. The ensuing dynasties in the main inherited these rules, making only some minor changes. Another distinguishing feature of men's costumes and adornments during the Tang Dynasty was a horizontal band attached to the lower part of the robe. The costumes of the four scholars in the painting "Literary Centre" by Han Huang show this feature, though the time was already quite close to the Five Dynasties.

Fig. 135 The gauze *fu tou* (rear view and profile) (Reconstruction based on ancient paintings and unearthed pottery figurines)

Fig. 134 The round-collared robe (Reconstruction based on ancient painting and unearthed pottery figurines)

82 Sui, Tang and the Five Dynasties

Fig. 136   An empereor in *fu tou* and round-collared robe with his attendants ("Imperial Carriage" by Yan Liben)

Fig. 137   Officials in *fu tou,* round-collared robes and black leather boots (Fresco from Li Zhongren's tomb, Qian County, Shaanxi Province)

Fig. 138   A late Tang official in *fu tou* and literary robe (Part of "Han Xizai's Evening Banquet" painting by Gu Hongzhong)

Fig. 139   Officials in *fu tou* and round-collared robes (Part of "Horseride Scroll", a Tang painting)

Fig. 140   A late Tang scholar in stiff-cornered *fu tou* and literary robe (Part of "Chess Game Behind Screens", painting by Zhou Wenju)

Fig. 141   A late Tang scholar in stiff-cornered *fu tou* and literary robe (Part of "Literary Centre" painted by Han Huang)

136

138

139

Sui, Tang and the Five Dynasties 83

137

140   141

84 Sui, Tang and the Five Dynasties

4. Women's Hairstyles

According to historical records, women's hairstyles in the Tang Dynasty included the "half-turned bun", the "reverse bun", the "happy-travelling bun", the "worried bun", the "lily bun," the "obedient bun", the "lingering bun", the "alerted swan bun", and the "double-ring fairy-viewing bun", all of which can still be seen from pottery figurines, frescoes, stone sculptures, stone carvings and ancient paintings.

The majority of the buns of the Sui were flat; the hair was combed into two or three layers piled up to form the shape of a hat. Although these styles were still popular in early Tang, the shape was not so smooth as in the Sui period since it tended to tower aloft. Later on, the buns got higher and higher, resulting in many new fashions. The most typical was the aristocratic ladies' "half-turned bun": the hair was usually set into one or two knife-shaped parts erected on the top of the head. The single knife-shaped part sloped to one side, whereas the double knife-shaped parts turned up from the two sides. During the days of Kai Yuan (Emperor Xuanzong's reign) the "double-ring fairy-viewing bun" and the "hui hu bun" became popular with common women, but these buns were not so high as the "half-turned bun". Ponytails were also quite popular among a small number of aristocratic ladies during the years of Tian Bao (Xuangzong's reign). Common women, however, preferred the "tossing-up bun", with the hair at the temples embracing the buns were made higher and higher, and were decorated with flowers, which heralded the popularity of the flowery hats of the early Song Dynasty.

142

143

144

Sui, Tang and the Five Dynasties   85

Fig. 142   Women's bun in the Sui Dynasty (White porcelain figurine, now in Shanghai Museum)

Fig. 143   Women's bun of mid Tang Dynasty (Part of "Beauties with Silk Fans", painting by Zhou Fang)

Fig. 144   Women's bun in the heyday of the Tang period (Coloured pottery figurine unearthed in Luoyang, Henan Province)

Fig. 145   Women's bun in the heyday of the Tang Period) (Part of "Washing White Silk" painted by Zhang Xuan)

Fig. 146   Women's bun of early Tang Dynasty (Drawing now in Tokyo Museum, Japan)

Fig. 147   Women's bun of the Five Dynasties (Part of "Han Xizai's Evening Banquet", painting by Gu Hongzhong)

145

146

147

5. Women's Makeup and Adornment

There are numerous beautiful lines in Tang poems describing women's makeup and adornment. For instance, we have "Applying face powder carefully layer upon layer, and putting rouge on the cheeks for a vision of loveliness", "A beauty with rouged cheeks and slender waist", "Learning to beautify both temples by applying dark yellow colour but not yet even half finished". "Drawing eyebrows with blue-black colour and making them fine and long", "Applying cosmetics skilfully to complete the facial decorations", "On the ground lay gold ornaments with no one to pick them up; kingfisher's wings, golden birds and hairpins of costly jade". Such lines reflect the great attention paid by women of the time to their appearance.

According to various records and literary sketches, a woman's makeup was usually done in the following order: first, apply powder; second, apply rouge; third, apply dark yellow cream; fourth, draw the eyebrows; fifth, apply lipstick; sixth, paint the cheeks; and seventh, apply the ornament between the brows.

White lead, one of the earliest cosmetics used in China, was first used during the period of the Xia and Shang Dynasties. It was said that the white lead (called *qian hua*) was so named because it was made from molten and pounded lead or tin. The rouge, also called *yang zhi* and produced in the Western Region, was mainly made from wild safflowers which grew profusely in the Yanzhi Mountains where the Huns lived. In the period of Sui and Tang, pomegranate flowers were sometimes used as a substitute. Before drawing eyebrows, women first shaved off their natural brows and then used a blue-black pigment made from charred osiers to draw whatever shape took their fancy. These were called *dai mei* (dark eyebrows). The shapes the Tang women invented ranged from the slender "beautiful eyebrows" to the wide "broad eyebrows", and in fact there were many variations. The so-called *hua dian* refers to a decoration between the eyebrows, said to have originated in the Southern and Northern Dynasties. One day, Princess Shouyang was sleeping under the eaves of the palace, when a plum flower fell accidentally on her forehead and dyed it. Try as she might, she could not wipe it off. The palace maids nevertheless marvelled at it and started to imitate. In the Tang Dynasty, *hua dian* was either painted or made of tiny metal pieces. A story tells that there was once an aristocratic woman who, in order to cover a mark on her cheek, painted something over it. Other women, not knowing her original intention, quickly followed suit; and soon, *mian ye,* as this kind of decoration was called, became a fashion.

148

149

Sui, Tang and the Five Dynasties 87

150

151

152

Fig. 148 A woman with *hua dian* decoration (Silk painting unearthed in Turfan, Xinjiang Uygur Autonomous Region)

Fig. 149 Tender-willow eyebrows (Silk painting unearthed in Turfan, Xinjiang Uygur Autonomous Region)

Fig. 150 A woman with *mian ye* on her cheek (Figurine with "clay head" and "wooden body" in costume, unearthed in Turfan, Xinjiang Uygur Autonomous Region)

Fig. 151 A woman with *dai mei* eyebrows (Part of "A Beauty with Flowery Hair Ornament", painting by Zhou Fang)

Fig. 152 A woman with *mian ye* on her cheek (Silk painting unearthed in Turfan, Xinjiang Uygur Autonomous Region)

88 Sui, Tang and the Five Dynasties

6. Jacket and Skirt, Short-sleeved Upper Garment and Cape

The jacket and skirt was the main dress style for Tang women. During the period of the Sui and early Tang, a short jacket with tight sleeves was worn in conjunction with a tight long skirt whose waist was fastened almost to the armpits with a silk ribbon. In the ensuing century, the style of this costume remained basically the same, except for some minor changes such as letting out the jacket and/or its sleeves.

As for women's skirts, there was quite a wide variety. The hundred-bird feather skirt, for instance, was once very popular among women of the middle and upper classes. Later, however, it was banned by the imperial court, because of the harm it caused to rare or auspicious birds. This did not affect the common women, since for them the fashion was the garnet skirt, so called because the skirt was of a bright red colour. In Tang novels, characters like Li Wa and Huo Xiaoyu were often portrayed in skirts of this kind. The skirts of the Tang Dynasty were novel, gay, delicate and beautiful, unequalled by anything produced in previous dynasties.

The short-sleeved upper garment derived from the short jacket. In general, it had a front opening and reached down to the waist where it was tied with a ribbon. There was also a "pull-over" style, which had a wider collar to bare the chest a little. To put it on, one just pulled it on over the head, either leaving the hems hanging outside or putting them inside the skirt in the manner of the short jacket.

The cape, also called the "drawing cape", was usually made of light, thin gauze printed with drawings or patterns. It was generally more than two metres long and was draped over the shoulders and twined between the arms. When the wearer was walking, the back-and-forth movements of the arms made the cape flow in a becoming manner.

Fig. 153 Short jacket, long skirt and cape (Reconstruction based on unearthed pottery figurines and frescoes)

Fig. 154 A woman of Sui Dynasty in narrow-sleeved short jacket and long skirt (Porcelain figurine of Sui Dynasty, now in Shanghai Museum)

Sui, Tang and the Five Dynasties 89

155

Fig. 155 Short jacket, long skirt and overgarment with turn-down collar and narrow sleeves (Reconstruction based on mural in Mogao Cave 303, Dunhuang)

90 Sui, Tang and the Five Dynasties

156

157 158 159

Sui, Tang and the Five Dynasties 91

160

Fig. 156 Short-sleeved upper garment with low-cut collar over jacket and skirt (Reconstruction based on unearthed pottery figurines)

Fig. 157-159 Women in jacket and skirt, short-sleeved upper garment and cape (Painted pottery figurines of Tang Dynasty, now in Shanghai Museum)

Fig. 160 Jacket and skirt together with short-sleeved upper garment (Reconstruction based on unearthed pottery figurines and frescoes)

92 Sui, Tang and the Five Dynasties

Fig. 161 Jacket and skirt with cape (Reconstruction based on an ancient drawing)

Fig. 162 A woman in short jacket and skirt together with cape (Part of "Beauties with Silk Fans", painting by Zhou Fang)

Fig. 163 A woman in jacket and skirt together with cape (Part of "Emperor's Favourite on Spring Excursion", painting by Zhang Xuan)

Sui, Tang and the Five Dynasties 93

164

165

166

Fig. 164 *Hu fu* with turn-down collar and front opening, striped trousers and leather belt (Reconstruction based on unearthed pottery figurines, stone carving and frescoes)

Fig. 165 A woman in *hu fu* and Tartar hat (Coloured pottery figurine unearthed in Xian, Shaanxi Province)

Fig. 166 A woman in *hu fu* with turn-down collar and wearing a bun (Coloured pottery figurine, now in Palace Museum, Beijing)

7. Hu Fu

Hu fu was very popular during the period of Kai Yuan and Tian Bao in Emperor Xuanzong's reign. The costume was characterized by its turned-down collar, front opening and tight sleeves, as may be seen in the frescoes and pottery figurines unearthed from the tombs of Wei Dong and Wei Xu in Xian as well as in the tomb of Princess Yongtai in Qian County, Shaanxi Province. Women in this Tartar dress are similarly shown in the Chinese classical paintings on silk unearthed in Asitana, Turfan, Xinjiang Uygur Autonomous Region. From these paintings, one can see that women in *hu fu* invariably wore a leather belt round their waists with several small ribbons hanging down. This kind of leather belt, originally the adornment of the northern tribes, was introduced into the Central Plains during the Wei and Jin period; and in the Tang Dynasty, it was once obligatory wear for both civil officials and military officers. Hung on the belt were seven objects, including a knife and a bag containing bamboo chips for purposes of calculation. It was not until the Kai Yuan period began, when new rules were set by the imperial court, that most officials were exempted from wearing such a belt. The belt remained popular among common women, only without the seven objects.

The belt also became narrower. As it no longer had any practical value, it was worn solely for decorative purposes.

94 Sui, Tang and the Five Dynasties

167

8. Large-sleeved Gown

In the heyday of the Tang period, the influence of *hu fu* weakened and, as a result, women's costumes became progressively more loose. Such a characteristic became particularly obvious in mid and late Tang, when the sleeve width of dresses worn by common women often exceeded four feet. Typical examples can be seen not only in the silk paintings of women unearthed at Mogao's Sutra Cave Library, Dunhuang, but also in Zhou Fang's painting of aristocratic ladies, "Beauties with Flowery Hairpins", and in the pottery figurines unearthed from two tombs of the Southern Tang period. The aristocratic ladies depicted in "Beauties with Flowery Hairpins" are the most characteristic. They have flowery hairpins for hair ornament and wear transparent gauze costumes without any underwear, except for a thin piece of gauze covering their bodies.

168

Sui, Tang and the Five Dynasties 95

169

Fig. 167 Dress style of large-sleeved silk gown with front opening, long skirt and cape (Reconstruction based on the painting "Beauties with Flowery Hairpins" and silk paintings unearthed in Dunhuang)

Fig. 168 An aristocratic woman in large-sleeved silk gown with long skirt and cape (Part of "Beauties with Flowery Hairpins" painting by Zhou Fang)

Fig. 169 Dress style of broad-sleeved gown with front opening, long skirt and cape (Reconstruction based on benefactor's costumes in Mogao Caves, Dunhuang)

96 Sui, Tang and the Five Dynasties

9. Costumes and Adornments of Female Dancers

In the Tang Dynasty, due to the emergence of a great number of distinguished scholars and artists, numerous works of art were produced, helping to promote dancing and music which also reached their zenith at this time. In addition to the inherited traditional dances, the northwestern Tartar dance also rapidly became popular across the country, resulting in a situation of "Everyone learning to dance, including officials and imperial concubines".

The Tang dances fell into two categories: the gentle and the dynamic. The latter was also called the "robust dance", while the former was called the "soft dance". Naturally, their movements were quite different from each other: the dynamic dance was intense and vigorous, while the gentle dance was like the sailing of a fairy. As the dynamic dance basically derived from the Tartar dance, the dancing costume was similar to *hu fu*. In general the sleeves were small so as to facilitate jumping and moving around. The gentle dance, on the other hand, was derived from the Han dance, and so the costume was usually large-sleeved, enhancing the mildness and smoothness of the dance itself.

The popularity of the Tartar dance had certain influence on the widespread acceptance of the *hu fu* during the periods of Zhen and Kai Yuan.

170

Fig. 170 Dancing costume (Reconstruction based on pottery figurines unearthed in Luoyang, Henan Province)

Fig. 171 A woman in dancing costume (Coloured pottery figurine unearthed in Luoyang, Henan Province)

Fig. 172 A woman in dancing costume (White porcelain figurine, now in Shanghai Museum)

Fig. 173 A woman in dancing costume (Yellow glazed pottery figurine, now in Shanghai Museum)

Fig. 174 A woman in dancing costume (Pottery figurine unearthed in Luoyang, Henan Province)

171

172

173

174

175

Fig. 175 Women in dancing costumes (Pottery figurines unearthed in Luoyang, Henan Province)

10. Hui Hu Costume

The Hui Hu, predecessors of the Uygurs, were a national minority in China's northwest region. During the Kai Yuan period, the Hui Hu developed the most powerful and prosperous regime among the northern national minorities. Nevertheless the Hui Hu people had close and friendly contacts with the Han people, so Hui Hu costume had considerable influence on the Hans, and was very popular with aristocratic ladies as well as women in the imperial court.

Hui Hu costume was somewhat similar in design to men's robes: it featured a turned-down collar, narrow sleeves, and loose body that reached to the ground. As for colour, warm shades were preferred, particularly red. With regard to material, thick brocade was generally used, and collar and sleeves were fringed with wide decorative brocade borders. To match this kind of costume, the wearer's hair was coiled up into the shape of a mallet, commonly called the "Hui Hu bun". The wearer then put on a peach-shaped hat embellished with jewellery, on top of which a phoenix was displayed. Hairpins were stuck in the hair at the temples, and earlobes and neck were also decorated with exquisite ornaments. For footwear, a pair of soft brocade shoes with raised head were usual.

Fig. 176 Hui Hu costume (Reconstruction based on Dunhuang Murals)

Sui, Tang and the Five Dynasties 99

177

178

Fig. 177 A late Tang aristocratic woman in Hui Hu bun, a golden phoenix hat and Hui Hu costume (Fresco in Yulin Cave, Anxi, Gansu Province. Copied by Zhang Daqian)

Fig. 178 A variant of the treasure-patterned brocade shoes with toe caps shaped in cloud patterns (Relic unearthed in Asitana, Turfan, Xinjiang Uygur Autonomous Region)

100 Sui, Tang and the Five Dynasties

179

11. Armour

Warriors of the Sui Dynasty chiefly adopted the Northern and Southern Dynasties' *ming guang kai* (shining armour), which usually had a curved collar, a shoulder cover and two round protective plates, one for the chest, and the other for the back.

Military costumes of the Tang, however, differed from those of previous dynasties. Historical records say that in the Tang Dynasty, "officers were clad in robes while soldiers wore jackets". From the period of Yan Zai onwards, the officers' robes were embroidered with designs of lions and tigers to suggest the bravery and might of the wearers. Nevertheless, the shining armour was still the main coat of mail, though there were some slight alterations in its structure. A knee-length skirt, for example, was added below the waist and a pair of suspended leg covers were attached to the shanks.

In the Tang Dynasty, combat armour was chiefly made from iron or leather. Among thirteen kinds of armour recorded in "The Six Codes of the Tang Dynasty", six (shining armour, shining waist armour, small-scaled armour, mountain-patterned armour, black hammer armour, and chain armour) were made of iron, mostly exquisitely shaped and wrought. The pieces were linked with leather strips or rivets. Other kinds of armour were mostly made of leather.

Apart from the iron and leather types, there were also "white cloth", "black silk" and "cotton vest" armour made of such fabrics as cotton and silk. Though light, easy to put on and of attractive appearance, they were unfit for combat purposes, and were only worn by officers in peace time or by the guard of honour. Finally, the cavalry and infantry wore armour made from wood. Styles of all the above-mentioned armour find expression in many extant paintings.

180

Sui, Tang and the Five Dynasties 101

Fig. 179 A warrior in helmet and coat of mail (Coloured sculpture in Mogao Cave 194, Dunhuang, Gansu Province)

Fig. 180 Dress style of helmet, coat of mail, and boots (Reconstruction based on unearthed pottery figurines and coloured sculptures)

Fig. 181 Dress style of helmet and coat of mail (Reconstruction based on unearthed pottery figurines)

102 Sui, Tang and the Five Dynasties

182

Fig. 182   A Tang warrior in silk armour (Coloured wooden figurine unearthed in Asitana, Turfan, Xinjiang Uygur Autonomous Region)

Fig. 183   A cavalryman in full armour (Colour pottery figurine unearthed in Asitana, Turfan, Xinjiang Uygur Autonomous Region)

Fig. 184   Imperial guards in embroidered robes (Mural in Mogao Cave 156, Dunhuang)

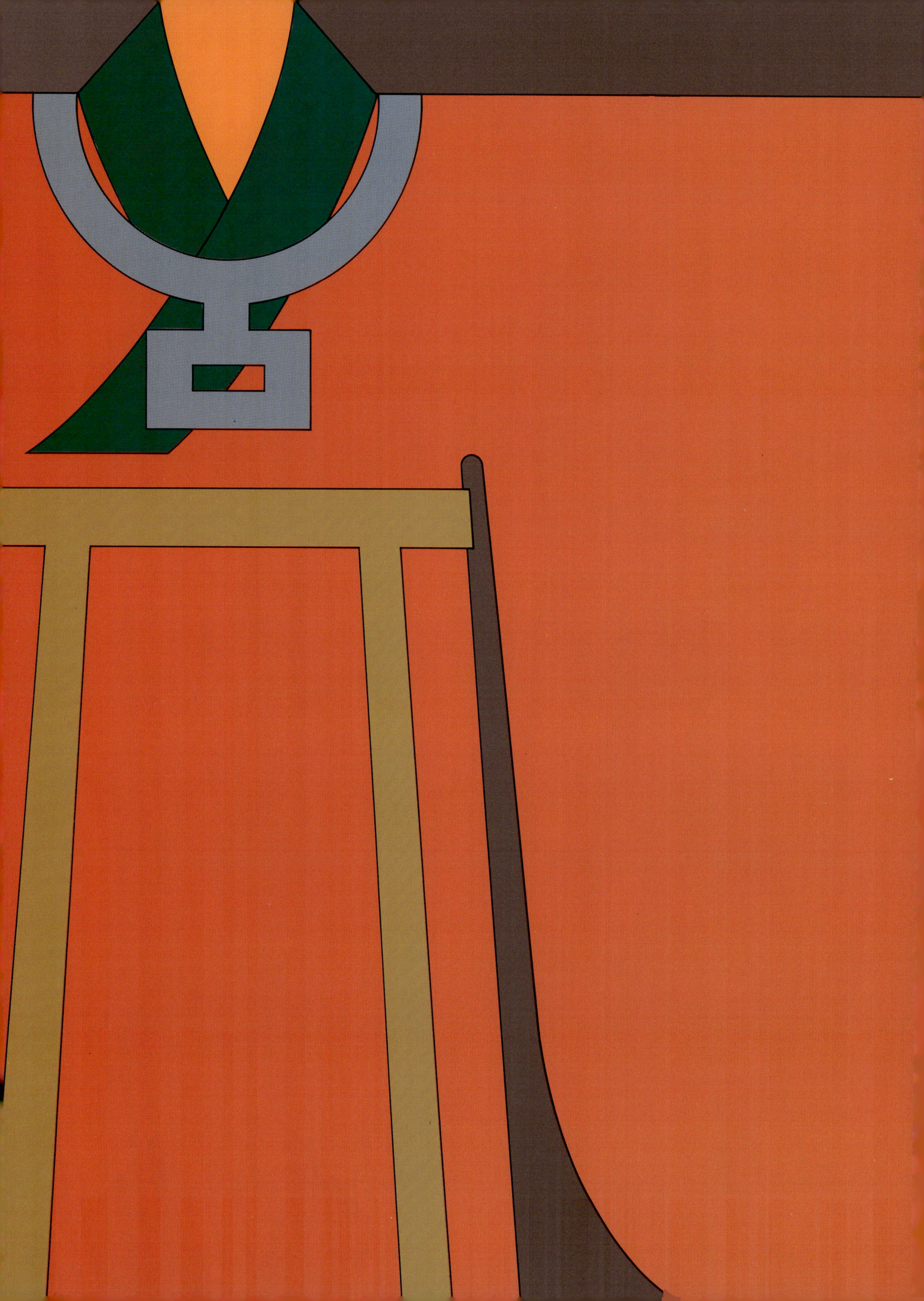

宋

SONG DYNASTY

The founding of the Song Dynasty by Zhao Kuangyin in A.D. 960 brought the disunity of the period of Five Dynasties and Ten States to an end, and China came under one ruler again. At the beginning of the Song Dynasty, the system of official and military ranks remained almost the same as during the Tang Dynasty, with only minor changes in the style of costumes. In the second year of Jian Long in Emperor Taizhu's reign (A.D. 961), the high-ranking scholar Nie Cengyi presented his "Three Protocol Graph" memorial to the throne, requesting a revision of the costume regulations, which was subsequently authorised by the Emperor. The graph contributed much to the formulation of the system for ceremonial costumes, and was looked upon as the blueprint for restoring the traditional dress system. There were several revisions of the dress code thereafter, the most extensive of which was carried out in the period of Da Guan and Zheng Ho (Emperor Huizong's reign). The protocol department devised a comprehensive system for dresses and caps in accordance with the ancient styles, and graphic illustrations were made for imitation in various regions.

The rise of idealist philosophy in the Song Dynasty had a great impact on the life of the people. Under the influence of this ideology, people's views on aesthetics changed considerably. In architecture, for example, whitewashed walls and black tiles came into fashion. Balustrades, pillars and roof beams were left unpainted so as to retain the true colour of the wood. In painting, also, simplicity and delicacy were valued, and the preferred medium was ink or light colours. The desire for simplicity was even more evidently reflected in clothing and related adornment, as public opinion was against excessive display in dress. Consequently, the clothing of the Song Dynasty was quite reserved and conservative, with fewer variations and quieter colours, thus conveying a feeling of simplicity and naturalness.

The *fu tou* (turban) of the Sui and Tang Dynasties had become the men's chief headgear by the Song Dynasty. From the emperor down to the multitude of civil officials and military officers, turbans were generally worn except when attending sacrificial rites, or important court sessions where coronets must be worn. The form of the turbans differed from that of previous dynasties, its most prominent feature being that the turban had evolved into a cap. On the back of this unique turban, there were generally two "feet", which were stuffed with supporting wire, string or bamboo strip, mounted with satin and gauze, and bent into various shapes. This accounts for such names as "straight feet", "curved feet" and "crossed feet". The first kind was mostly used by emperors and officials, and the second and third by attendants, various public servants and messengers, and musicians, who were of low social status. The turban originally had a rattan lining inside and was covered with gauze outside, a coat of paint being applied to give resistance to wear and tear. Later, since the paint and gauze was considered strong enough, the rattan lining was omitted, and the cap was consequently called the "paint-and-gauze turban".

Compared with the *fu tou* of Sui and Tang, the *fu tou* of the Song Dynasty had other variations: In Sui and Tang, the *fu tou* was generally made of black gauze, whereas the *fu tou* of the Song Dynasty was not strictly confined to that colour. On special occasions such as weddings and banquets, bright colours were also allowed. Some turbans even had gold silk threads wound into various patterns and mounted on top.

Since the turban had evolved into a cap worn by all civil officials and military officers, it was seldom used by the masses. Scholars and students in general reinstated the "Wrapping turban" of ancient times and thought it very graceful. This kind of wrapping turban was called a Dongpo (Scholar's) wrapper, and had a high crown and short brim. There were also other wrapping turbans with names such as "Scholar Chen's wrapper", "valley wrapper", "high scholar wrapper", and "unrestrained wrapper". By the Southern Song Dynasty, the wrapping turban had become even more prevalent, and high officials at court were also in the habit of wearing it. In consequence, the system governing the coronet gradually sank into oblivion.

Men's dress of the Song Dynasty, official dress for government personnel included, was still mainly the robe with round collar. Robes were usually worn by officials except on such occasions as sacrificial rites. The robes were of different colours — purple, crimson, red, blue or green to show the wearer's rank. Officials in purple (of the sixth rank and above) or crimson robes must have "fish pockets" of gold and silver hung across their waists. This regulation originated in the Tang Dynasty. The pocket was first used to hold a "fish tally" — a fish-like ornament made of copper used as a proof of identity for officials in central and local governments — which later became a badge to designate the official's position. It was three Chinese inches long, with Chinese characters carved on it, and was split into two halves: one was kept in the central government, and the other in the local government. In the case of promotion, correspondence between the two halves of the "fish tally" was necessary as evidence. The pass for entering or leaving the palace gate or city gate was similarly fish shaped and was also called the "fish tally". In fact it was a variation of the "tiger tally", but the form of a fish was adopted in order to avoid using the name of one of Emperor Gaozu's ancestors. Furthermore, as a fish's eyes are open day and night, they symbolized "constant vigilance", which is why the "fish tally" was used as a pass. According to the regulations of the Tang Dynasty, all officials above the fifth rank were granted fish pockets to hold their tallies. Although the fish tally was no longer in use by the time of the Song Dynasty, the fish pocket was not discarded; and it was considered a great honour to "wear purple with a fish pocket". When officials of low ranks had unusual missions to perform (diplomatic missions, for instance), they had to wear the fish pocket and were required to borrow a purple or crimson robe before going on these missions — this was called "borrowed purple" or "borrowed crimson".

The hairstyle of the women of the Song Dynasty still followed the fashion of the later period of the Tang Dynasty, the high bun being the favoured style. Women's buns were often more than a foot in height. Some of the young women's buns were combed into a "heavenward" style, as shown in the coloured statue of court attendants in the Holy Mother's Palace inside the Jin Temple in Taiyuan, Shaanxi Province. To dress this type of high bun, switches were generally used, sometimes fashioned into switch buns of various shapes, coiled directly on top of the head. This was called a "coronet of special buns". Women from rich families, however, usually had hairpins and combs made into the shape of flowers, birds, phoenixes, or butterflies to be pinned on top of the buns.

Another kind of headgear in vogue was called the "coronet comb", and was a kind of high coronet made of painted yarn, gold, silver, pearls or jade, with two flaps hanging down over the shoulders, and a long comb of white horn erected on top. As the combs were nearly one foot long and the two sides were heavy with ornaments, the wearer had to turn her head sideways when entering a carriage or passing through a door. This kind of coronet was very much in fashion in the Northern Song Dynasty, and is accurately depicted in Dunhuang murals.

It was also customary at this time to pin flowers on the coronet. Inheriting the fashion of the Tang, women of the Song Dynasty made artificial flowers from satin or the stem of the "rich-paper" plant, or from gold, silver, pearls and emerald hawksbill. Some of the flowers copied were peach, apricot, lotus, chrysanthemum and plum. Some even grouped the flowers together and mounted them on the coronet, calling this arrangement "all-year-round scenery". And such a custom was not confined to women alone: on grand occasions such as festive rites and important court gatherings, the emperor and his officials also wore flowers to ornament their headgear. The custom is reflected in a verse line, written in a playful tone: "Multifarious peonies and roses, blooming on the caps of a thousand officials".

When the women of the Song Dynasty went out, they wore a "head cover", presumably a derivation of the *mi li* (a kind of turban). Women also wore this headdress on their wedding day to veil their faces. The veil should be gently lifted by the emissaries of the bridegroom's family to reveal the "flowery face". This convention lasted all through the Ming and Qing Dynasties. Detailed descriptions of it can often be found in Chinese novels or plays.

Women's upper garments consisted mainly of coat, blouse, loose-sleeved dress, over-dress, short-sleeved jacket and vest. The lower garment was mostly a skirt.

The jacket was chiefly worn by women of the lower class. Coats were generally worn in winter and blouses in summer. The blouses were generally made of silk or satin. The over-dress was the ordinary dress for women in the Song Dynasty, worn by everyone, from the empress and imperial concubines, down to servants, attendants, slave actresses, and musicians. It was also worn by men, but mostly inside the official dress. The short-sleeved upper garment and waistcoat were fundamentally identical, being the costume for commoners. Both had a front opening, but the former had sleeves while the latter was sleeveless.

The styles of women's skirts in this period were retained from previous dynasties, and varieties included the "garnet skirt", the "double butterfly skirt" and the "embroidered satin skirt". There were aristocratic women who had their skirts dyed in tulip juice. When worn, the skirts emitted a gush of fragrance, which accounted for their great popularity. After the Northern Song, however, the style of skirts underwent some slight changes. The width of most skirts increased more than sixfold and there were fine ruffles in the middle, historically called "a hundred folds" or "a thousand folds". Such skirts had a silk belt fastened around the waist and a ring of ribbon hanging down.

As for the colours of women's costumes in this period, upper garments were usually of quiet, mixed colours, such as light blue, whitish purple, silver grey and bluish white. For skirt, strong colours were used, such as green, blue, white, and apricot-yellow.

Women in the Song Dynasty seldom wore boots, since binding the feet had become fashionable. It would have been quite inconvenient to wear boots, so women had shoes made of satin or silk and embroidered with various designs. Amongst these were the "embroidered shoes", the "brocade shoes", the "phoenix shoes", and the "gold-thread shoes", referred to as the "gold lotus" by poets and essayists.

The armour of the Song Dynasty on the whole followed the system of late Tang and the Five Dynasties period, and changes, if any, were insignificant. With the rapid development of firearms since the Southern Song, armour gradually fell out of use.

108 Song Dynasty

1. Emperor's Court Dress

The high crown and gauze robe were worn by the Emperor on highly significant occasions such as grand court sessions and major title-granting ceremonies, when officials wore their corresponding costumes. The emperor's high crown was called the "curling-cloud crown", and was adorned with 24 "curly beams", each about one foot in height, and one foot in width. Mounted in the front of the crown were a gold ornament and decorations made of gold or hawksbill in the shape of a cicada. The colour of the crown was blue outside and red inside. When worn, it was pinned on the hair with hairpins made of jade or rhinoceros horn. The gauze robe was crimson in colour, with patterns of clouds and dragons embroidered in red and gold, and black borders stitched onto collar, sleeves, lapels and hems. A red gauze skirt and knee covers were fastened around the waist. White yarn underwear was worn inside. A necklet with a pendant (round top and square bottom) was hung around the neck and an elegant belt with ribbons was tied to the waist. The emperor wore white stockings and black boots.

Fig. 185 Crimson gauze robe, knee cover and round necklet with square pendant (Reconstruction based on Historical documents and "Portraits of monarchs of Various Dynasties" exhibited in Nanxun Palace)

Fig. 186 *Zhong dan* (unlined garment worn under the robe) (Reconstruction based on historical documents and "Portraits of Monarchs of Various Dynasties" exhibited in Nanxun Palace)

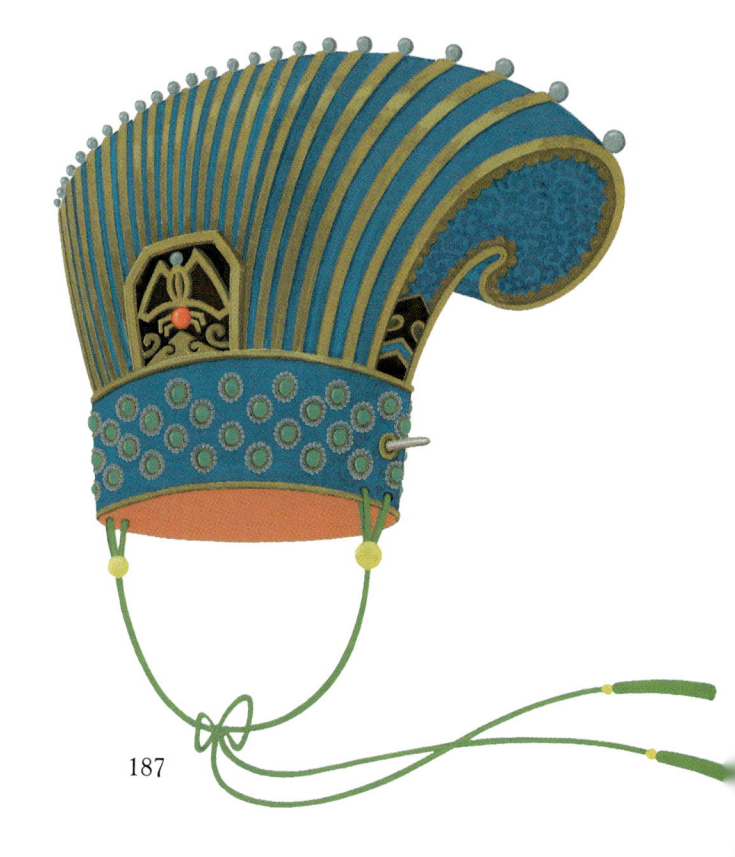

Song Dynasty 109

186

Fig. 187 The high crown (Reconstruction based on historical documents and "Portraits of Monarchs of Various Dynasties" exhibited in Nanxun Palace)

188

Fig. 188 The black boots (Reconstruction based on historical documents and "Portraits of Monarchs of Various Dynasties" exhibited in Nanxun Palace)

Fig. 189 An emperor in high crown, crimson gauze robe and round necklet with square pendant ("Portraits of Monarchs of Various Dynasties" exhibited in Nanxun Palace)

189

110　Song Dynasty

190

2. Empress' Ceremonial Dress

The empress wore the *hui yi* (the empress' upper garment) on grand occasions such as title-granting by the Emperor and sacrificial rites. The regulations were the same as those codified in "Book of Rites of Zhou", the *hui yi* was made of dark blue *zhi cheng* (a kind of woven fabric) decorated with a pattern of coloured pheasants. The collar, sleeves, lapels and full front were fringed with a red material decorated with patterns of clouds and dragons. When wearing this kind of dress, the empress must also wear a phoenix crown, blue yarn inner garment and dark blue knee cover hanging from the waist. She also wore a pair of jade pendants and other jade ornaments. Blue stockings and shoes completed the outfit.

191

Fig. 190 Ceremonial dress for the empress (Reconstruction based on "Portraits of Empresses of Various Dynasties" exhibited in Nanxun Palace)

Fig. 191 An empress wearing a dragon-phoenix crown adorned with pearls and emeralds (Reconstruction based on "Portraits of Empresses of Various Dynasties" exhibited in Nanxun Palace)

Fig. 192 Officials' formal dress; turban with outstretched "feet"; and large girdle with jade embellishments (Reconstruction based on paintings, unearthed pottery figurines and stone carvings)

Song Dynasty 111

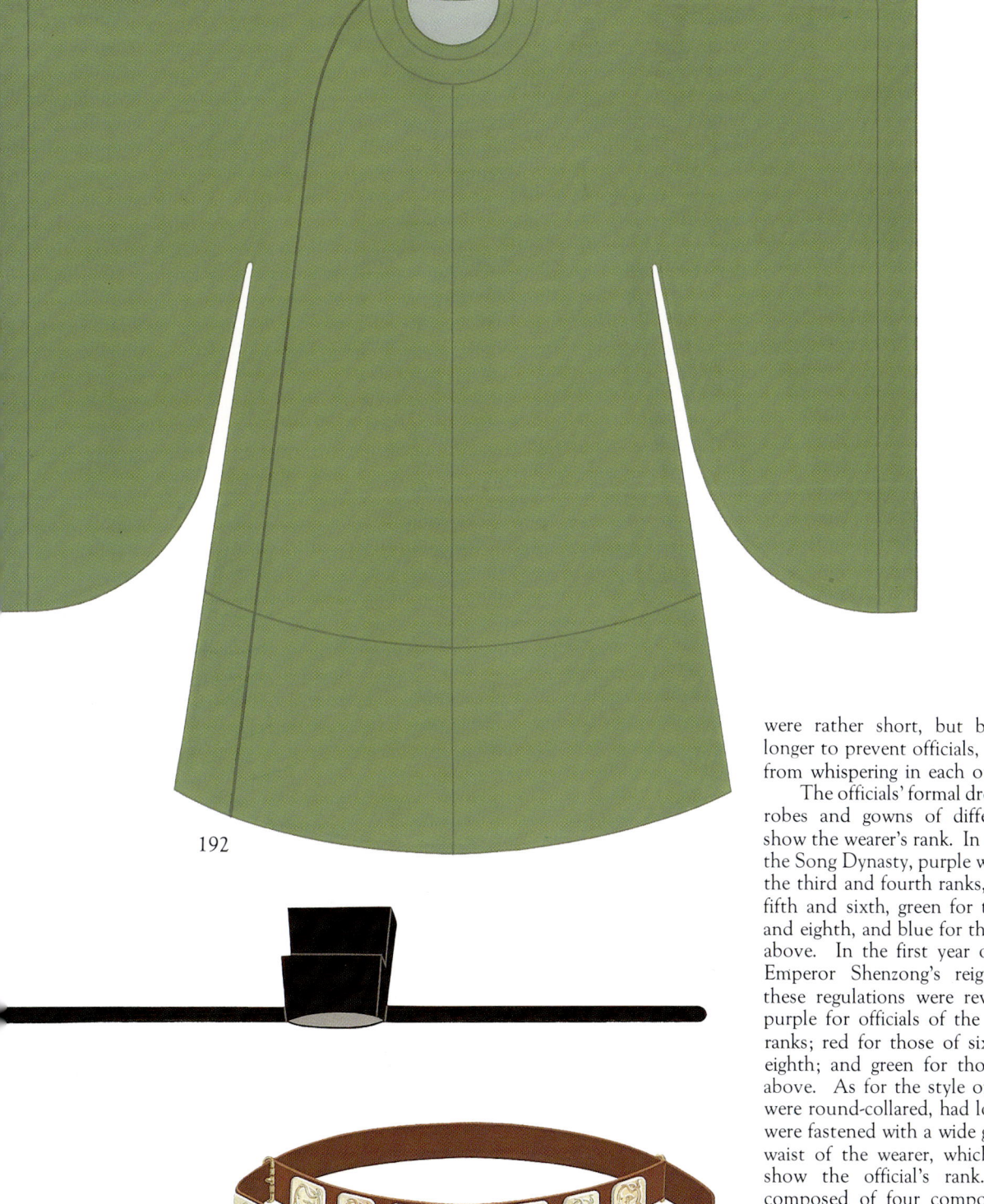

192

3. Formal Dress for Officials

According to Song regulations, all officials must wear formal dress during routine court sessions, while on important occasions such as sacrificial rites and court meetings, they must wear the sacrificial dress or the court dress. The turban which was worn with the formal dress was mostly fashioned with hard wings, which at first were rather short, but became gradually longer to prevent officials, or so it was said, from whispering in each other's ears.

The officials' formal dresses were mainly robes and gowns of different colours to show the wearer's rank. In the early years of the Song Dynasty, purple was for officials of the third and fourth ranks, red for those of fifth and sixth, green for those of seventh and eighth, and blue for those of ninth and above. In the first year of Huan Feng in Emperor Shenzong's reign (A.D. 1081), these regulations were revised as follows: purple for officials of the fourth and fifth ranks; red for those of sixth, seventh and eighth; and green for those of ninth and above. As for the style of the robes, they were round-collared, had loose sleeves, and were fastened with a wide girdle around the waist of the wearer, which also served to show the official's rank. The belt was composed of four component parts: two strips of leather, ornamental pieces, buckle and two metallic ends, one worn in the front and the other at the back. The one in front had punched holes for insertion of the buckle and was embellished with gold and silver at both ends. The one at the back was decorated with a row of square or round ornamental pieces, the number and quality of which depended on the wearer's rank. According to regulations, the one with ornamental pieces must be worn at the back, while the two metallic ends should face downward as a sign of obedience to the court.

112 Song Dynasty

193

4. Costumes for Scholars

Dress for the scholars in the Song Dynasty mainly consisted of gowns made from fine, white cloth, with folds around the waist. There were also the "purple gowns", the "cool gowns" and the "cap-matched gowns". The purple gowns were originally worn by cadets. They were convenient to wear, and became ordinary garb for scholars first, and later for officials and military officers. The cool gowns, similar to the purple gowns, were also called white gowns, and first were used as ordinary dress for officials, later becoming the apparel for mourning. Cap-matched gowns were ordinary social dress for scholars, the cap being made of gauze and the gowns of satin. Collars might be round or crossed, the latter being the more popular. There were also people who preferred the front opening. All these can be seen in such paintings by Song artists as "Philosophizing In the Shade of the Pine Trees", and "Listening to Music". In addition, actual examples have been discovered in large numbers. In the tomb of Zhou Yu in Jintan, Jiangsu Province, for instance, many such dresses have been unearthed.

194

Song Dynasty 113

195

196

197

Fig. 193 An official in soft "feet" turban cap and round-collared gown (Part of "Listening to Music", painting by Zhao Jie)

Fig. 194 White unlined gown with round collar (Relic from Zhou Yu's tomb in Jintan, Jiangsu Province)

Fig. 195 Lacquered gauze fu tou (Relic from Zhou Yu's tomb in Jintan, Jiangsu Province)

Fig. 196 Silk shoes with patterns of water caltrops (Relic from Zhou Yu's tomb in Jintan, Jiangsu Province)

Fig. 197 Lined jacket with front opening and embellished with a peony flower and twisted branch (Relic from Zhou Yu's tomb in Jintan, Jiangsu Province)

114 Song Dynasty

Fig. 198 A scholar in turban and gown (Part of "Portrait of (Wang) Xizhi (the Calligrapher)", painting by a Song artist)

Fig. 199 White gauze unlined garment with front opening (Relic from Zhou Yu's tomb in Jintan, Jiangsu Province)

Fig. 200 Broad-sleeved garment (Reconstruction based on Song paintings, pottery figurines and unearthed artifacts)

5. Broad-sleeved Garment

The broad-sleeved garment was originally the ordinary dress for empresses and imperial concubines. Later, aristocratic women used it as a ceremonial form of dress. Commoners, however, were not allowed to wear this kind of garment and were required to wear the overdress instead. Broad-sleeved garments can be seen on murals in Mogao Caves, Dunhuang, and in frescoes in Sanqing Hall, Yongle Palace. In recent years, articles of this kind have also been found in tombs of the Southern Dynasty found in Fuzhou region, Fujian Province.

116 Song Dynasty

201

202

203

Song Dynasty 117

204

205

Fig. 201 Broad-sleeved gown of satin gauze and long skirt (Reconstruction based on frescoes in Yongle Palace)

Fig. 202 A woman in phoenix crown, gown and skirt, wearing pendant (Fresco in Sanqing Hall, Yongle Palace, Shaanxi Province)

Fig. 203 Gold hairpin with phoenix head (Artifact disinterred in Baoshan County, Shanghai)

Fig. 204 Broad-sleeved gown with front opening, cape and long skirt (Reconstruction based on costumes worn by benefactors in murals in Mogao Caves, Dunhuang)

Fig. 205 Aristocratic women in coronet-comb, broad-sleeved gown, long skirt and cape (Mural in Mogao Cave 61, Dunhuang)

118 Song Dynasty

206

207

Fig. 206 White satin gauze broad-sleeved garment (Artifact from Huang Shen's tomb of Southern Song Dynasty, Fizhou, Fujian Province)

Fig. 207 Part of white satin gauze broad-sleeved garment (Artifact from Huang Shen's tomb of Southern Song Dynasty, Fuzhou, Fujian Province)

Song Dynasty 119

6. Over-dress

The over-dress was an ordinary dress, quite popular among the women of the Song Dynasty. Its style was mainly that of paired front pieces, which were often left open, i.e., not fastened with buttons or strings, thus revealing the clothing inside. The dress usually reached over the knees, and in some cases it was as long as the skirt. Slits, more than two feet long were opened at the sides, a feature rarely seen in other dresses.

A fresco in a Song tomb unearthed at Baisha, Yu County, Henan Province, shows several maids holding trays with cups of water or toilet articles, or directly helping their mistress — an aristocratic woman — to fix her hair and make-up. Most of these young women can be seen in over-dresses. Also dressed in this kind of costume are the maids of honour sculptured within the Holy Mother Hall in the Jin Temple, Shaanxi Province. Many of the artifacts found in the tombs of aristocratic women of the Southern Song Dynasty also testify to the popularity of the over-dress during that period.

Fig. 208 Over-dress (Reconstruction based on brick carving and pottery relief)

Fig. 209 Women in over-dress (A fresco from a Southern Song tomb at Baisha, Yu County, Henan Province)

120 Song Dynasty

Fig. 210 Over-dress made from crepe fabric (From Huang Shen's tomb of Southern Song in Fuzhou, Fujian Province)

Song Dynasty 121

7. Jacket and Skirt

The jacket was formerly a piece of underwear which was not revealed. In the Tang Dynasty this short jacket was once the main upper garment for women. It was adopted in the Song Dynasty without modification and used as the ordinary dress for women. Since it was close-fitting, it was convenient for work wear and was, therefore, very popular among women of the lower class.

In the Holy Mother Hall in Jin Temple, Shaanxi Province, there are quite a few coloured sculptures of maids of honour in short jackets and skirts, the style being identical to that depicted in the late Tang painting "Evening Banquet of Han Xizai". Only the location of the opening was optional; it could be either on the right or on the left, chiefly owing to the influence of the northern Khitan and Nuzhen nationalities. In the middle of the skirt there was a streamer attached to a round jade ornament. The purpose of wearing such an ornament was to weigh down the hem of the skirt to prevent it from fluttering in the wind when walking, which was considered to be essential for good manners.

Fig. 211 Narrow-sleeved short jacket, long skirt and cape (Reconstruction based on stone carvings, coloured sculptures and patterns of existing articles)

Fig. 212 Women wearing hairpins, short jacket and skirt, and cape ("The Imperial Concubine Bathing Her Baby Son", painting by a Song artist)

Song Dynasty

Fig. 213 Aristocratic women wearing hairpins, short jackets and skirts, and capes served by a maid dressed in a gown ("Leisure in Autumn", by a Song artist)

Fig. 214 A maid of honour in short jacket with narrow sleeves (Coloured sculpture in Holy Mother Hall of Jin Temple, Taiyuan, Shaanxi Province)

Fig. 215 A maid of honour in jacket and skirt, with cape (Coloured sculpture in Holy Mother Hall of Jin Temple, Taiyuan, Shaanxi Province)

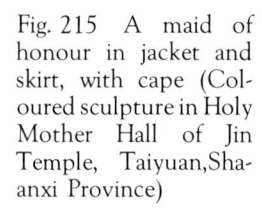

Fig. 216 A maid of honour in jacket and skirt, with cape, and wearing jade pendant (Coloured sculpture in Holy Mother Hall of Jin Temple, Taiyuan, Shaanxi Province)

Song Dynasty 123

Fig. 217　Pleated skirt made of printed satin gauze (From Huang Shen's tomb in Fuzhou, Fujian Province)

Fig. 218　Skirt with hem fringed with decorative satin borders (From Huang Shen's tomb in Fuzhou, Fujian Province)

8. Costumes of the Common People

In the Song Dynasty, there were also regulations governing costumes for the common people. In the book "Happy Dreams" we read the following account:

"There were hierarchical differences between the costumes of people of various callings, such as scholars, peasants, workers and businessmen. Clerks in incense shops wore caps and over-dresses; pawnshop keepers wore wrapping turbans, black gowns and cornered girdles; and street peddlars wore dresses of specific colours to signify their trades".

From what is recorded in this book, it can be seen that the Northern Song capital Bianjing (present-day Kaifeng, Henan Province) was full of restaurants and teahouses. Commercial firms of each trade formed themselves into "business associations". In the costume and adornment business alone there were dozens of such business associations: the existence of associations for the hat trade, the shoe trade, the jewellery trade, the silk girdle trade, the collar trade, the haberdashery trade, the headdress trade, the headgear-repair trade, the comb-dyeing trade and the laundry trade, reflects the prosperity of business in those days. Such a thriving scene is vividly depicted in the famous painting "Spring Excursion". In this exquisite work of art, people from all walks of life can be seen; officials, gentlemen, pedlars, peasants, doctors, petty officials, polers, towing men, cartmen, boatmen, monks, Taoists and many others. They are dressed in many different kinds of costumes. Some go bare-headed, others wear buns, or turbans of different sorts, or straw hats; some wear gowns, others are in over-dresses or unlined upper garments. The painting records all the basic features of the costumes worn by the common people in the Song Dynasty.

Song Dynasty 125

Fig. 219, 220 Common people in various costumes (Part of the painting "Spring Excursion", by Zhang Zheduan)

Fig. 221 Peasants in head scarves, wearing short jackets and trousers (Part of "Weaving and Ploughing", painting by a Song artist)

126　Song Dynasty

9. Armour

The armour of the Song Dynasty followed the regulations of late Tang and the Five Dynasties in the main with only minor revisions. The Northern Song's "Military Encyclopaedia", records in detail the styles and the governing regulations for armour in the Northern Song Dynasty. For instance, it was specified that the warrior should wear a helmet, armour, protective covers for shoulders and arms, and leggings for the lower limbs. The half-length stone statue unearthed at Yuncheng, Shaanxi Province, and the pottery soldiers unearthed from Southern Song tombs in Chengdu, Sichuan Province, compare well with the forms recorded in the "Military Encyclopaedia". With the steady development of firearms from the Southern Song onward, armour gradually fell out of use.

222

Fig. 222　A suit of armour (Reconstruction based on wooden and pottery figurines and Song paintings)

Song Dynasty 127

Fig. 223 A warrior in full armour (Coloured statue in Mogao Cave 55, Dunhuang)

Fig. 224 Warriors in full armour (Part of "Three Visitations to the Thatched Cottage", painting by a Song artist)

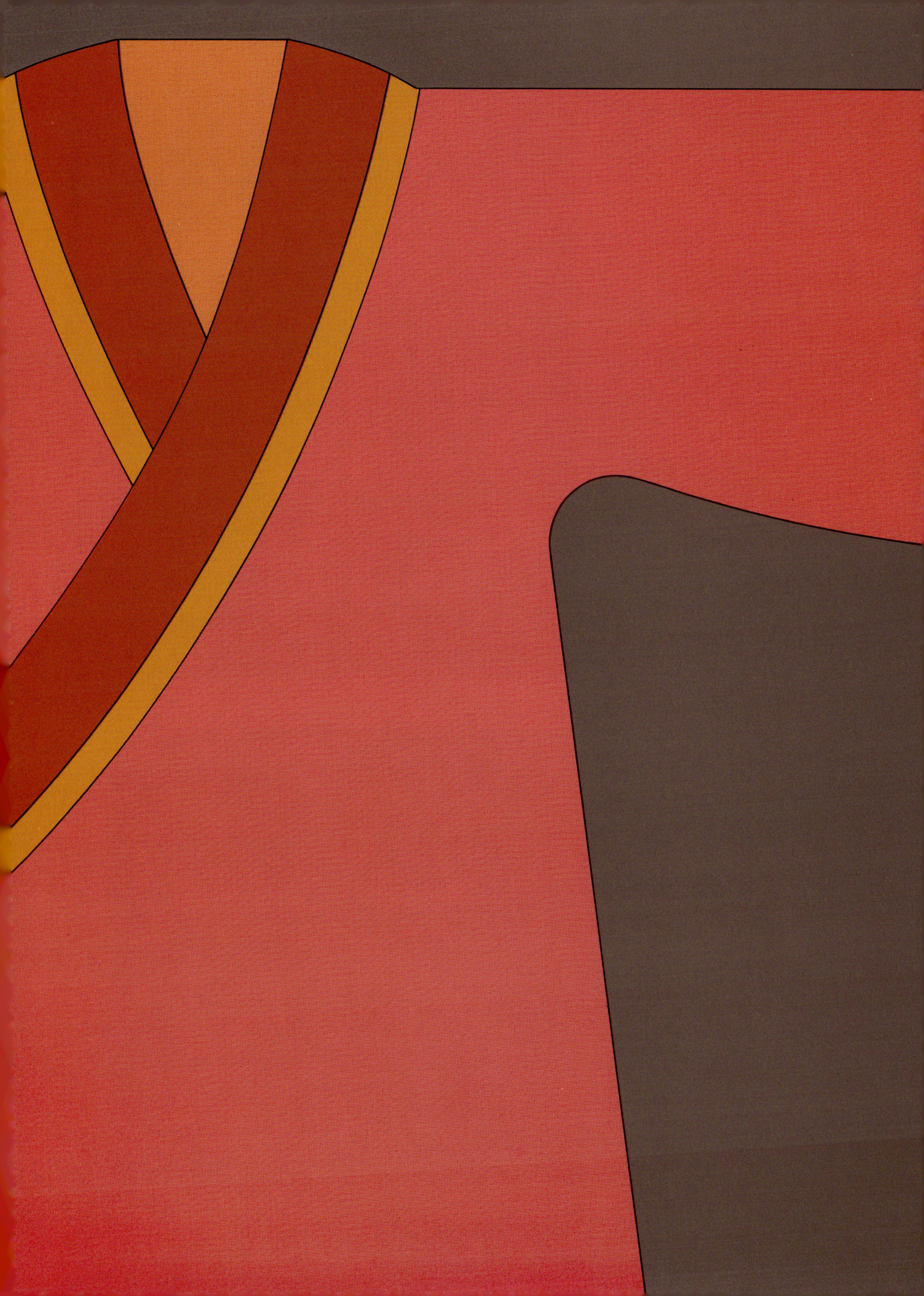

遼金元

LIAO, JIN AND YUAN DYNASTIES

The three dynasties of Liao, Jin and Yuan were chiefly national minority regimes, established respectively by the Khitan, Nuzhen and Mongol tribes, all of whom were originally inhabitants of the northern parts of China. The economic and cultural exchanges they conducted with the Han people were also reflected in their costumes.

When Emperor Taizu proclaimed himself ruler of Liao in the north, only armour was worn in the court, as the nomads had had no particular tradition in costume. But when the Khitans marched south into the territory of Later Jin, they came under the influence of the Han people and consequently also set up regulations for costumes. Two types of clothing were in use simultaneously during this period: native Khitan clothes for officials of Khitan origin, and Han costumes for Han officials, who inherited the systems of late Tang and the Five Dynasties.

In the reign of Qian Heng (A.D. 979-982), some changes in the costume system took place, and Khitan officials, too, began to wear Han costumes, though this was only for grand ceremonial occasions and only officials of the three highest ranks were privileged to wear them.

For everyday wear, there were two systems: the Emperor and officials of Han birth wore Han costume; while the empress and officials of Khitan birth wore Khitan costume.

Regulations for headgear in Liao differed from those of previous dynasties. Only the emperor and his highest ministers had the right to wear a hat or kerchief. As for officials of the middle and lower ranks and common people, they were strictly forbidden to wear any headgear even in private, so that they had to go bareheaded even in winter.

According to Khitan customs, men shaved the crown of their heads, leaving only a little hair for ornament at the temples and over the forehead. Some people had their hair cut short on the forehead in a straight line, others let the hair at the temples hang loosely to the ears, and still others trimmed the side tresses into specific forms and let them flow freely on either side over the shoulders.

Women's hairstyles were simpler. They dressed their hair in a high bun, a twin bun, or a spiral bun. Some women wore their hair loose, with a band or a kerchief around the forehead. Others wore a small hat in the form of an upturned bowl, decorated with a sash that floated behind.

Robes were the main form of dress for both men and women, nobles and commoners. The emperor wore white silk at sacrificial rites and a green flower-patterned tight gown for ordinary occasions. The empress wore a seamed red linen robe, while courtiers wore tight gowns or embroidered robes. All the robes were buttoned on the lefthand side. They were round-necked, with tight sleeves, and were mostly of dark, serene colours. Robes worn by the aristocracy were elaborately made, as evidenced by a cotton-padded robe unearthed in Liaoning Province, which has smooth embroidery upon a background material of brown muslin with two figures of dragons on the collar. On the shoulders, chest and around the waist are embroidered fairies with flower hairpins, riding phoenixes and designs of peaches, smartweed, waterbirds and butterflies.

The costumes of the Jin Dynasty in the main followed the system of the Nuzhen people, but official dress took over the Liao traditions. After conquering the northern territory of Song, Jin formulated its own codes corresponding to the Song systems. From the second year of the reign of Tian Chun (A.D. 1139) onward, all officials were required to wear court costume at court gatherings with the emperor. In the third year of Tian Chun, a complete code for costumes was formulated. Prescribed in detail were not only the emperor's crown and court dress and the empress' coronet and costume, but also the formal and everyday wear of officials of every rank. In the seventh year of the reign of Huang Tong (A.D. 1147), costumes for officials to wear at sacrificial rites were further specified. Then, in the third year of Da Ding (A.D. 1163) costumes were designed for officials to wear when discharging their duties, thus completing the system.

The hairstyles of the Jin Dynasty were entirely different from those of the Liao. Men now wore long hair plaited and trailing over their shoulders, while women coiled up their plaited hair into buns. Older women liked to cover the buns with a black hair net, on which jade ornaments were pinned in a random arrangement. The net was therefore called *xiao yao jin* or "random kerchief".

The everyday wear for men of the Nuzhen nationality consisted of four parts: black turban, circular-collared robe, belt made of jade, gold or rhinoceros horn, and black leather boots.

The choice of colour was typical of the Nuzhen tribe. Being a nomadic people, they carefully dressed themselves in the colour of their environment for better self-protection, as well as to disguise themselves in order to approach their prey unnoticed in hunting. Fur was more frequently used than textiles for better resistance against cold winds and snowstorms.

Young women liked to wear jackets of black, purple or dark reddish colour, with dark purple skirts to match. The jackets were usually straight-collared and buttoned on the left-hand side, while the pleated skirts were embroidered with flowers on whole branches. Red and yellow ribbon held the skirt at the waist and hung freely down to the wearer's feet. Later, owing to the influence of the Hans, the *bei zi* (vest) was also introduced. The

Jin *bei zi* was slightly different from that of the Song Dynasty, since it was usually parted in the middle, the front piece just reaching the ground, while the back piece trailed behind for about five Chinese inches.

The Yuan Dynasty was also founded by a nomadic people with a poorly developed economy and culture, which accounted for the simplicity of their clothing. Influenced by the lifestyle of the Han people on the Central Plains which they conquered, they too became more and more richly dressed, and eventually they also established a complete system for costumes.

Both the Mongols and Nuzhens wore their hair in plaits, but in different ways. The Mongols first parted their hair in the middle of the crown to form a cross ($\otimes$), then shaved the hair on the back of the head, trimmed the hair in the front into various shapes (oblong, angular, or peachlike) and let it hang naturally over the forehead, and finally plaited the hair on either side of the cross and tied it into a ring that reached the shoulders.

Headgear for men of Han birth in the Yuan Dynasty was as follows: working costumes for officials were matched with *fu tou,* which on the whole resembled those of the Song Dynasty. The *fu tou* were made of lacquered gauze and had two tails stretching out on either side. Attendants and servants wore them upturned and those worn by gentlemen and scholars, following the Tang model, had their two tails slanting down behind the head to form the Chinese character "八" (eight). Commoners wore a turban styled according to personal preference. Mongolian men wore corrugated hats made of rattan strips, but there were also some who preferred bamboo hats. Women of the Mongolian aristocracy wore a kind of hat called *gu gu guan.* Han women, however, usually combed their hair into buns and few of them wore hats.

The robe was again the predominant costume in the Yuan Dynasty, but it was much broader than the Liao robe. Working costumes for officials were made of muslin after the Han model, with loose sleeves, circular collar, and buttons on the left-hand side, and body length usually reaching the toes. Different colours were used to denote differences in rank.

Zhi sun (one-colour clothes) were costumes for the emperor and his courtiers of all ranks — with respective specifications for each — at festive court banquets. Made of a particular kind of brocade, *zhi sun* had a rich variety of styles, each with its specific patterns and ornaments. For the emperor alone, there were 26 different styles. Even for civil and military officers the styles also numbered more than twenty. In everyday life both the nobility and commoners wore tight-sleeved gowns, occasionally with a short-sleeved over jacket, as was the case with servants and attendants.

The robe was also the chief garment for Mongolian women, and was mostly buttoned on the lefthand side. The cuffs were tight, and under the robe over-trousers were worn, which had neither waist nor crotch, but were simply trouser-legs tied to the belt. Many examples of such clothing have been found in Yuan tombs in Shandong Province.

Han women continued to wear the jacket and skirt. However, the choice of darker shades and buttoning on the left showed Mongolian influence.

For footwear during this period, Han people adhered to the systems of Tang and Song, while men and women of the northern tribes kept to boots.

132   Liao, Jin and Yuan Dynasties

1. Costumes of Liao Dynasty

The robe was the garment for both men and women. Men's robes were tight-sleeved and round-collared, and opened on the left. The front lapels were connected by buttons, and the waist was tied with a silk band flowing down to the knees. Sombre colours, such as grey-green, grey-blue, brown and dark green, were preferred; and the designs on the fabrics were usually very simple. Beneath the robe was a shirt, the collar of which came above that of the robe and whose colour was of a lighter shade, such as white, yellow, light green, beige or light grey. The over-trousers were strapped to a waistband and the trouser-legs were tucked into high leather boots. Women's robes were mostly buttoned on the left, cross-collared and tied at the waist with a silk band. Many women wore skirts; these, however, were mostly concealed beneath the robe. Women also wore high boots. The styles of the above-mentioned costumes are vividly illustrated in the drawing "*Zuo Xie tu*"(relaxation). In this painting, men have shaved hair and only the influential wear kerchiefs. The women wear their hair in spiral buns with a sash tied over the forehead. Only one lady of the aristocracy has a bowl-shaped hat. The portrayals agree perfectly with the descriptions found in historical documents. Another picture, "Eighteen Stanzas to the Hu Reed Pipe", attributed to a painter of the Song Dynasty, tells the story of Cai Wenji's return to her motherland years after her marriage to a Hun ruler. In the picture the costumes worn by the Huns bear a close resemblance to those of the Khitans, reflecting the custom of that period.

Fig. 225 Round-collared robe (Reconstruction based on paintings and unearthed frescoes)

225

Fig. 226 Khitan horsemen in round-collared robe (Fresco from liao Tomb No. 1 in Kulun Banner, Zhelimu League, Jilin Province)

Fig. 227 Hair-shaved Khitan aristocrats wearing round-collared robes with tight-sleeves (Part of the painting "Back from a Hunting Trip" attributed to a Song painter)

134 Liao, Jin and Yuan Dynasties

Fig. 228 Tight-sleeved robe with left opening (Reconstruction based on drawings and frescoes)

Fig. 229 Khitan women in tight-sleeved robes with left opening and men in round-collared robes (Part of the painting "*Zuo Xie Tu*" (relaxation) by Hu Huai)

Liao, Jin and Yuan Dynasties 135

Fig. 230 Horsemen in round-collared robes (Part of the painting "*Zuo Xie Tu*" (relaxation) by Hu Huai)

Fig. 231-232 Khitan men and women in tight-sleeved robes (Part of the painting "Eighteen Stanzas to the Hu Reed Pipe" attributed to Chen Juzhong)

136 Liao, Jin and Yuan Dynasties

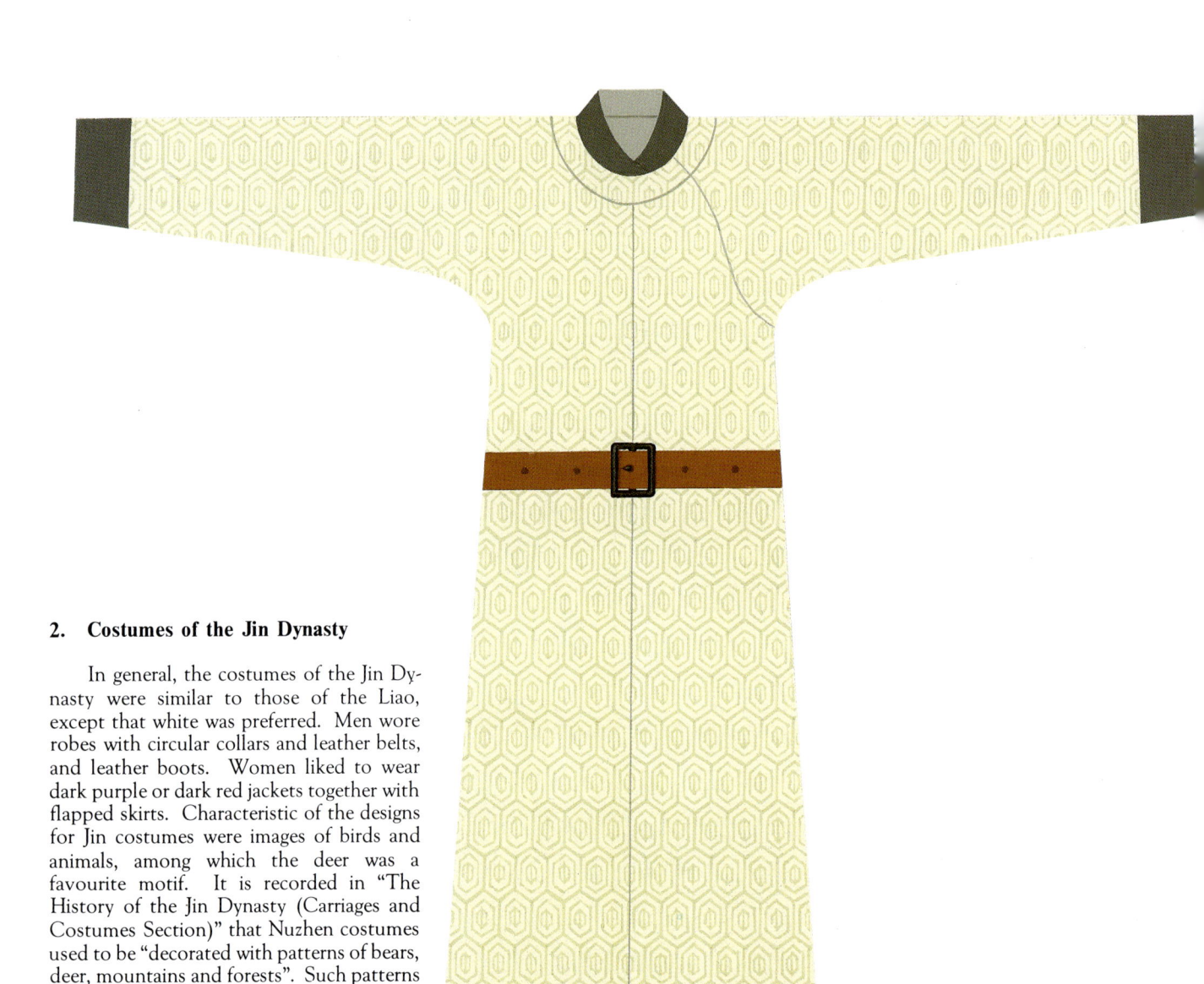

2. Costumes of the Jin Dynasty

In general, the costumes of the Jin Dynasty were similar to those of the Liao, except that white was preferred. Men wore robes with circular collars and leather belts, and leather boots. Women liked to wear dark purple or dark red jackets together with flapped skirts. Characteristic of the designs for Jin costumes were images of birds and animals, among which the deer was a favourite motif. It is recorded in "The History of the Jin Dynasty (Carriages and Costumes Section)" that Nuzhen costumes used to be "decorated with patterns of bears, deer, mountains and forests". Such patterns are also seen in the jade and brick carvings excavated from Jin tombs. The unique shapes of deer depicted at leisure or in flight, bring out the rich flavour of the life of the nomads.

233

Fig. 233 Round-collared robe with tight sleeves (Reconstruction based on unearthed brick carvings)

Liao, Jin and Yuan Dynasties 137

Fig. 234 Dress style of tight-sleeved robe with left opening and long skirt (Reconstruction based on unearthed brick carvings and pottery figurines)

138 Liao, Jin and Yuan Dynasties

235

3. Gold Brocade Dragon Robe

After the founding of the Yuan Dynasty, the Mongols were strongly influenced by the customs and life style of the Hans. One of the most conspicuous instances of this is their adoption of dragon and phoenix patterns.

A creation of the Han people, the dragon and phoenix patterns were a symbol of Chinese culture. From late Tang and the Five Dynasties onward, such patterns were inherited in succession by one regime after another of the northern national minorities. The designs achieved even greater prominence in the Yuan Dynasty, when they were no longer confined to costume, but found expression even in architecture, furniture, carriages and banners.

Besides pattern, the costumes of the Yuan aristocracy were also distinguished by their numerous shades of colour. Brown, for instance, had more than 20 different shades, including "golden tea brown", "autumn tea brown", "eaglewood brown", "onion white brown", "pale lilac brown" and "grape brown". Some patterns had glittering gold thread woven into them to make the costume more opulent.

236

Liao, Jin and Yuan Dynasties   139

Fig. 235 Gold brocade dragon robe, palm hat, cloud-patterned cape and satin boot (Reconstruction based on drawings, pottery figurines and unearthed artifacts)

Fig. 236 Emperor in fur and attendants in gold brocade (Part of "Kublai Khan on a Hunting Trip", by Liu Guandao)

Fig. 237 Half-sleeved gold brocade costume (Reconstruction based on drawings)

Fig. 238 An aristocrat in headress and gold brocade robe (Drawing)

140   Liao, Jin and Yuan Dynasties

4. Square Corrugated Hat and Plaited Garment

Mongolian men wore hats made of rattan strips, called *wa leng mao* or corrugated hats, which were round or square in shape. In general, ornaments were set on the top of the hats, and for the noble and rich, the ornaments usually consisted of jewels.

The plaited garment was a long robe with circular collar, tight sleeves and body portion which flared from the waist down and was pleated with dense folds. A broad band made of plaited threads was sewn to the waist, hence the dress was also called the "lined-waist garment". Appearing first in the Jin Dynasty, the costume can be seen on pottery figurines found in Jin tombs in Jiaozuo County, Henan Province. In the Yuan Dynasty the garment was so widespread that people of humble status such as attendants and guards were also allowed to wear it. This is borne out by the entry "Apparel for Guards" in "The History of the Yuan Dynasty (Carriage and Costume Section)".

Fig. 239 Plaited garment, square corrugated hat and leather boot (Reconstruction based on Yuan Dynasty block-printed books and pottery figurines)

Fig. 240 A man in corrugated hat and plaited garment (Pottery figurine unearthed in Jiaozuo, Henan Province)

5. Costumes for Aristocratic Women

According to Yuan Dynasty regulations, the *gu gu guan* (coronet) was the headdress for the empress, concubines of the emperor, and wives of high ministers; while fur hats were worn by commoners. The *gu gu guan* was originally a hat about two Chinese feet high, made of birch bark and covered on the outside with black cloth, or red silk for the rich. The hat was decorated at the top with willow branches 4-5 feet long, or wires wrapped in blue felt, together with flowers, coloured silk and pheasant feathers. An elaborate depiction of it is found in "Portraits of Emperors and Empresses of Various Dynasties".

The *gu gu guan* was matched with a big robe with loose sleeves and a train so long that it had to be held up by maids walking behind the wearer. Images of this are frequently seen in the murals of mogao Grottoes in the Dunhuang and Yulin Caves in Anxi.

Fig. 241 Cross-collared gold brocade robe (Reconstruction based on costumes of Yuan Dynasty benefactors depicted in Dunhuang Murals and "Portraits of Emperors and Empresses of Various Dynasties")

Fig. 242 An empress in *gu gu guan* and cross-collared gold brocade robe (From "Portraits of Emperors and Empresses of Various Dynasties" in Nanxun Palace)

142   Liao, Jin and Yuan Dynasties

6. Jacket and Skirt and Half Sleeve Over-jacket

After the Mongols settled down in the Central Plains, Mongolian customs and costumes also had their influence on those of the Han people. While remaining the main costume for Han women, the jacket and skirt had deviated greatly in style from those of the Tang and Song periods. Tight-fitting garments gave way to big, loose ones; and collar, sleeves and skirt became straight. In addition, lighter more serene colours gained preference. Iconographic records show a half sleeve jacket over the two-piece suit, girdled at the waist with an apron and tied with flowing ribbons. Drawings of this are seen in the Cunyang Hall frescoes, Yongle Palace, Shaanxi Province and in the Water God Temple of Guangsheng Monastery in Hongdong County of the same province.

243

Liao, Jin and Yuan Dynasties 143

244

Fig. 243-244 Jacket and skirt and half sleeve over-jacket — front and rear views (Reconstruction based on frescoes in Water God Temple of Guangsheng Monastery, Hongdong County, Shaanxi Province)

Fig. 245 A maid in a colourfully decorated hat, jacket and skirt, and half sleeve over-jacket (Fresco in Water God Temple of Guangsheng Monastery, Hongdong County, Shaanxi Province)

245

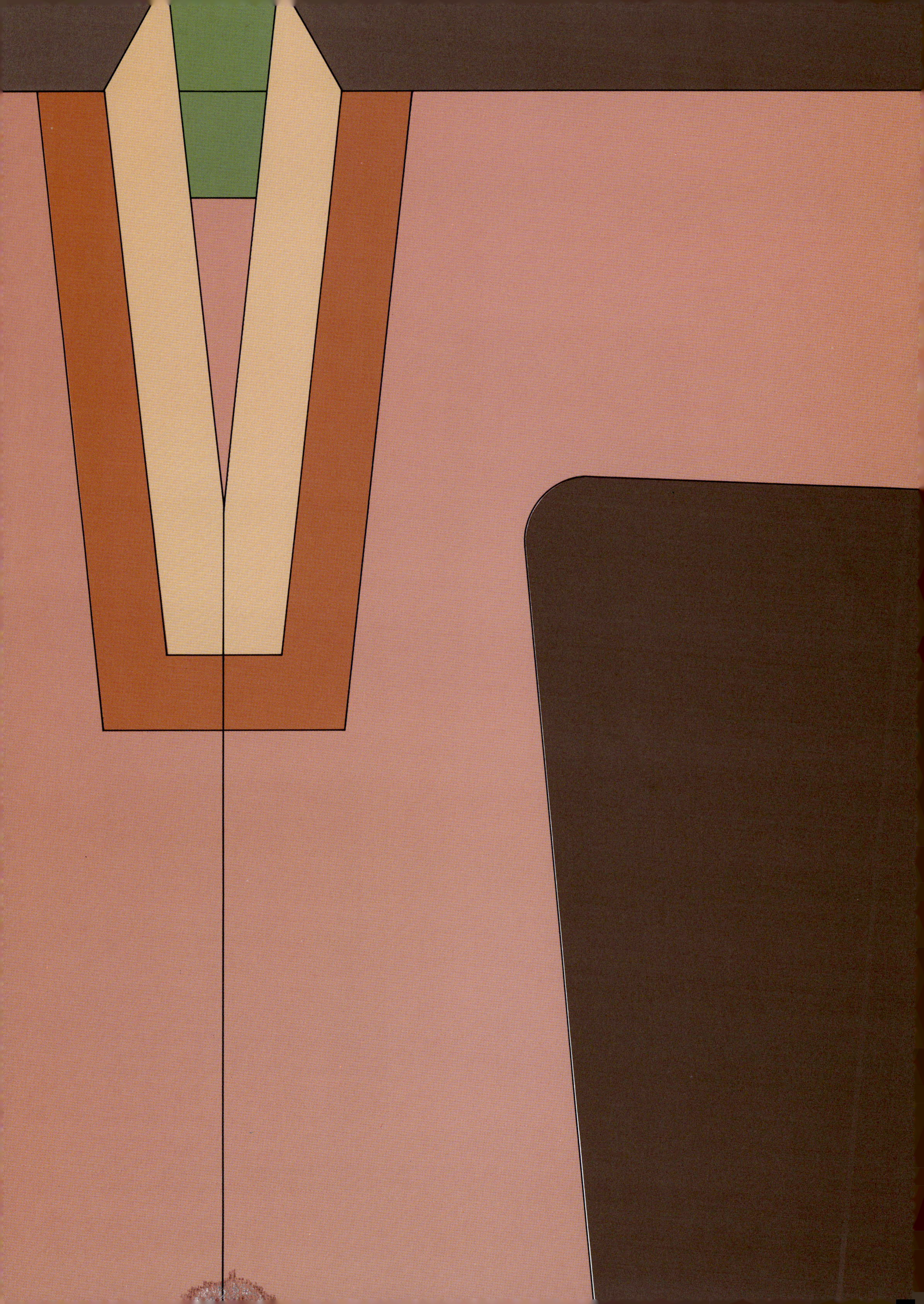

明

MING DYNASTY

After the founding of the Ming Dynasty, the rules and regulations for costumes set by the Yuan Dynasty were abolished, and, following the custom of the Han people, the dress system underwent large-scale reform resulting in the restoration of the Han costumes — those of Zhou and Han Dynasties and those of Tang and Song Dynasties. The changes took more than 20 years to implement, and it was not until the 26th year of Hong Wu (A.D. 1393) in Emperor Taizu's reign that a new set of costume regulations was codified.

The men's turban styles of the Ming Dynasty consisted mainly of the black gauze cap, *fu tou*, the net turban, the quadrangular flat-topped turban, and the "six-in-one" cap.

In the Ming Dynasty it was customary for officials to wear black gauze caps during routine court sessions. The *fu tou* was worn at important court meetings, and when reporting to the throne or giving thanks to the emperor. The shape of the *fu tou* was the same as during the Song Dynasty, but was characterized by the fact that its two ends were stretched apart like straight rulers. The net turban was a kind of net hood that bound the hair-buns, and was knitted of fine black strings, horsetail, and fine palm fibre. Wearing a net turban was not simply for keeping the hair in position, but also marked the age of manhood. A number of net turbans were commonly worn inside coronets, but they could also be used singly. The quadrangular flat-topped turban cap, made primarily of black satin, was the ordinary cap for officials and scholars. Since it had right-angles at the four corners, it was also called the "quadrangular turban". The six-in-one cap, commonly called *gua pi mao* (small round skullcap), was a patchwork of six scraps of gauze and was mostly worn by commoners. Other caps for men of the Ming Dynasty were the "high scholar's turban", the "loyalty coronet", and the "sun-shading cap".

The clothing for men of the Ming Dynasty marked a revival of traditional features, and the gown was their fabourite costume. Court attire for officials inherited old-time regulations, which required the wearing of coronets or caps and formal costumes. The regulations for court wear were as follows:

In such important ceremonies as sacrificial rites, all civil officials and military officers, whatever their rank, were required to wear coronets with stripes and costumes of red satin. Ranks were differentiated by the number of stripes mounted and the kind of ribbon worn on the girdle:

1st rank: coronet with seven beams; leather girdle ornamented with jade; ribbon embellished with a 4-colour motif of clouds and phoenix.

2nd rank: coronet with six beams, leather girdle ornamented with rhinoceros horn; same ribbon as for the 1st rank.

3rd rank: coronet with five beams, leather girdle ornamented with gold; ribbon with motif of clouds and crane.

4th rank: coronet with four beams, the rest the same as for the 3rd rank.

5th rank: coronet with three beams, leather girdle ornamented with silver; ribbon with motif of a perching eagle.

6th or 7th rank: coronet with two beams, leather girdle with silver ornament; ribbon with 3-colour motif of a magpie.

8th or 9th rank: coronet with one beam, leather girdle with black horn; ribbon with 2-colour motif of mandarin ducks.

Regulations for the breast tablet were also designated: those for 1st through 5th ranks were made of ivory, and those for 6th through 9th of locust tree wood.

Public dress for officials was the gown, the regulations being: circular collar and right opening; sleeve — 3 *chi* (Chinese foot) wide; made either of linen or of satin gauze. The designated colours were 1st through 4th ranks — crimson; 5th and 6th — blue; 8th and 9th — green. The gowns were embroidered with different patterns appropriate to specific ranks, and were mostly worn on important occasions, with *fu tou* to match.

When attending routine court sessions, an official generally wore his ordinary dress, which also fell into the public dress category, though the system was simpler. It generally consisted of a black gauze cap, a circular-collared upper garment, and a leather girdle. In the 26th year of Hong Wu, it was ordained that officials must wear the over-gown as their ordinary dress. Such over-dresses were adorned with embroidered square patches, with a pattern of birds for civil officials and beasts for military officers. Again, distinctions were made for all the nine ranks as a means of marking hierachical levels.

Costumes and accessories for men of other social classes were also designated: government servants of various sorts wore lacquered cloth coronets adorned with peacock plumes. Round their waists the men wore knitted girdles of red cloth. Constables, who were of lower status, wore small caps, blue garments with outer waistcoats of red cloth and blue knitted girdles. The rich merchants, wore dresses made of silk or satin, and gauze and carefully avoided being too conspicuous by restricting their choice of colour to blue or black. However, to distinguish themselves from servants and government officials, they decorated their collars with white gauze or satin.

Women's hairstyles in early Ming were in the main the same as those of the Song and Yuan Dynasties; but from the years of Jia Jing onward, they became more and more varied. For instance, there was the "peacock bun" — hair combed flat and circular, with precious stones pinned on top in flowery patterns. Then there was a style which involved combing the hair high, lacing it up with gold and silver strings, and decorating it with pearls and emeralds. Seen from a distance, it looked like a man's gauze cap. Still another style was an imitation of a popular Han Dynasty bun called "falling-off-the-horse bun". The hair was coiled upwards and laced into a large bun that dangled behind the head. Apart from these hairstyles, there was also the switch bun, which was no less popular. The switches were made on a ring fastened with iron wire in a style prevalent in ancient times. Serving as a set adornment called a "drum", the false hair was one and half times as high as ordinary buns, and it was fastened on the top with hairpins. By the end of the Ming Dynasty, the styles of switches had become even more varied, the prominent ones being the "arhat bun", the "idler's bun", "the pair of flying swallows", and the bun that "loosened on touching the pillow". Some of these buns were ready-made and were available in jewellery stores; they remained popular even in the early years of the Qing Dynasty.

Young women in the Ming Dynasty also wore hair clasps. The material originally used was palm fibre, which was shaped into a net to hood the hair. Clasps made of yarn and satin appeared afterwards, and the shape changed often, being wide in the beginning and becoming progressively narrower. By early Qing, it had been transformed into a narrow strip fastened onto the forehead. The so-called "marten hood over the forehead" and the "fishwoman's tie" were names used for these embellishments.

The clothing for women in the Ming Dynasty consisted mainly of gowns, coats, rosy capes, over-dresses with or without sleeves, and skirts. These styles were imitations of ones first seen in the Tang and Song Dynasties. However, the openings were on the right-hand side, according to the Han Dynasty convention.

With regard to titled women (mothers and wives of officials), regulations for their costumes were also rigidly codified. There were two main kinds of attire: formal and informal. The former was worn by titled women when they were having an audience with the empress, meeting their uncles, aunts or husbands, or attending sacrificial ceremonies. The outfit was composed of the phoenix coronet, the rosy cape, the loose-sleeved blouse, and the over-garment. Specific regulations for material, colour, pattern and measurement, were Laid down in detail in "*Ming Hui Dian*" (an encyclopaedia of rules and regulations produced during the Ming Dynasty), and variations from them were prohibited. For example, the colour of a loose-sleeved blouse could only be crimson, and that of a sleeveless embroidered mantle or over-dress could only be dark blue. Measurements were also given for each part of the formal dress: the length of the blouse's frontal piece — 4.12 *chi*, the back piece — 5.1 *chi*; sleeve-length — 3.22 *chi*. The rosy cape for titled ladies had two strips, each measuring 5 *chi* in length and 0.32 *chi* in width. The informal dress refers to the titled women's everyday wear, primarily in the form of a long coat and a long skirt. Regulations for there being less strict, all sorts of gauze, satin or silk could be used, and only patterns and border decorations were stipulated.

The formal dress for commoners could only be made of coarse purple cloth, and no gold embroidery was allowed. Gowns could only be in such light colours as purple, green and pink; and in no case should crimson, reddish blue or yellow be used. These regulations were observed for over a decade, and it was not until the 14th year of Hong Wu that minor changes were made.

As to footwear, officials wore boots or "cloud toe shoes" (commonly called "court shoes"), while scholars and students often wore black "double-vamp shoes". The majority of commoners wore ordinary shoes, and in the southern regions most people wore straw sandals. The weather in the northern provinces being cold, people there generally wore leather boots with vertical stitches; while women, mostly with bound feet, wore "bow shoes" with high soles made of camphor wood. The shoes with exterior wooden soles were called "external high soles" or "fragrant leaves", "lotus seeds", or "lotus flowers". Shoes with interior soles were called "internal high soles" or "Taoist priest's coronets". Older women frequently wore flat-soled shoes called "fragrance on the surface of the soles".

The armour used in the Ming Dynasty was mostly made from copper or iron, but seldom leather. The rank and file also wore armour made of metal when in combat.

1. Emperor's Ordinary Dress

The ordinary dress for the emperor, commonly called the "dragon robe", was made of yellow satin embroidered with dragon patterns and pheasant designs. When wearing the dragon robe, the emperor also wore the "turn-up gauze turban", the shape being basically the same as that of the black gauze cap, differing only in that the corners on the right and left were lifted upwards to the back of the gauze cap. A detailed depiction of this coronet can be seen in the painting "Portraits of Monarchs of Various Dynasties" exhibited in the Nanxun Palace. The emperor's gold crown excavated at Ding Ling (one of the imperial tombs of the Ming Dynasty outside Beijing) is also of this type.

Fig. 246 Dragon robe (Reconstruction based on descriptions in "*Ming Hui Dian*" and the painting "Portraits of Monarchs of Various Dynasties" exhibited in Nanxun Palace)

Fig. 247 Gold crown with turn-up turban (Relic from Ding Ling)

248

Fig. 248 An empereor in circular-collared robe with narrow sleeves (From "Portraits of Monarchs of Various Dynasties" exhibited in Nanxun Palace)

2. Empress' Ceremonial Dress

The ceremonial dress of the empress was composed of the phoenix crown, rosy cape, pheasant garment, over-dress and loose-sleeved blouse. The phoenix crown was made on a framework of wires, on which an imitation of a phoenix was mounted and strings of pearls and precious stones were hung. The crown had been the head ornament of the abdicated emperor's wife, the empress dowager and the crowned empress ever since the Qin and Han Dynasties. In the Ming Dynasty, there were two kinds of phoenix crowns: one was for the empress and the imperial paramours, being decorated with dragons and multi-coloured pheasants, together with phoenixes. The empress' crown was embroidered with nine dragons and four phoenixes, and that of the paramours had nine multi-coloured pheasants and four phoenixes. The other kind, called a coloured coronet, was worn by titled women, and it was not adorned with dragons or phoenixes, but with pearls, plumes of wild fowls, and flowery hairpins.

The rosy cape looked like two coloured chains circling the neck and allowed to hang over the breast with pendants of gold and jade on their ends. This form of adornment appeared as early as in the Northern and Southern Dynasties and it became increasingly popular in the Sui and Tang Dynasties. People likened it to a beautiful rainbow and it was thus called 'xia pei' (rosy clouds cape). In his poem "The Dance of Rainbow and Feather Garments", the Tang poet Bai Juyi wrote, "Rainbow costume and rosy cape, with coronet on the head rocking with ornaments stuck to the hairpins". The rosy cape was used as a component part of formal dress in the Song Dynasty, and its embellishments were determined according to rank. It was inherited without modification in the Ming Dynasty, and was used as ceremonial dress for titled women.

249

250

251

252

253

Fig. 249 Pheasant garment (Reconstruction based on records in "*Ming Hui Dian*" and paintings in "Portraits of Empresses of Various Dynasties" exhibited in Nanxun Palace)

Fig. 250 Knee cover (Reconstruction based on records in "*Ming Hui Dian*" and paintings in "Portraits of Empresses of Various Dynasties" exhibited in Nanxun Palace)

Fig. 251 Rosy Cape (Reconstruction based on records in "*Ming Hui Dian*" and paintings in "Portraits of Empresses of Various Dynasties" exhibited in Nanxun Palace)

Fig. 252 Empress' Dragon and Phoenix crown adorned with pearls and emeralds (From excavations at Ding Ling, Beijing)

Fig. 253 An empress in phoenix crown and rosy cape (From "Portraits of Empresses of Various Dynasties" exhibited in Nanxun Palace)

154 Ming Dynasty

257

258

259

260

Fig. 257-258 Square patches embroidered with *xi li* for civil officials of seventh rank (From tomb of Zhu Cuncheng in Songjiang County, Shanghai)

Fig. 259-260 Square patches embroidered with orioles on front and back pieces of the same robe (From tomb of Pan Yunzheng in Zhaojiabang Lu, Shanghai)

Fig. 261 A robe embroidered with unicorns (Drawing based on unearthed artifact)

Fig. 262 An official in black gauze *fu tou* and robe with pattern of python embroidered in gold ("Portrait of Li Zhen" by a Ming artist)

Fig. 263 Hair-tying jade coronet

Fig. 264 Jade buckle and hook

Fig. 265 Jade hairpins

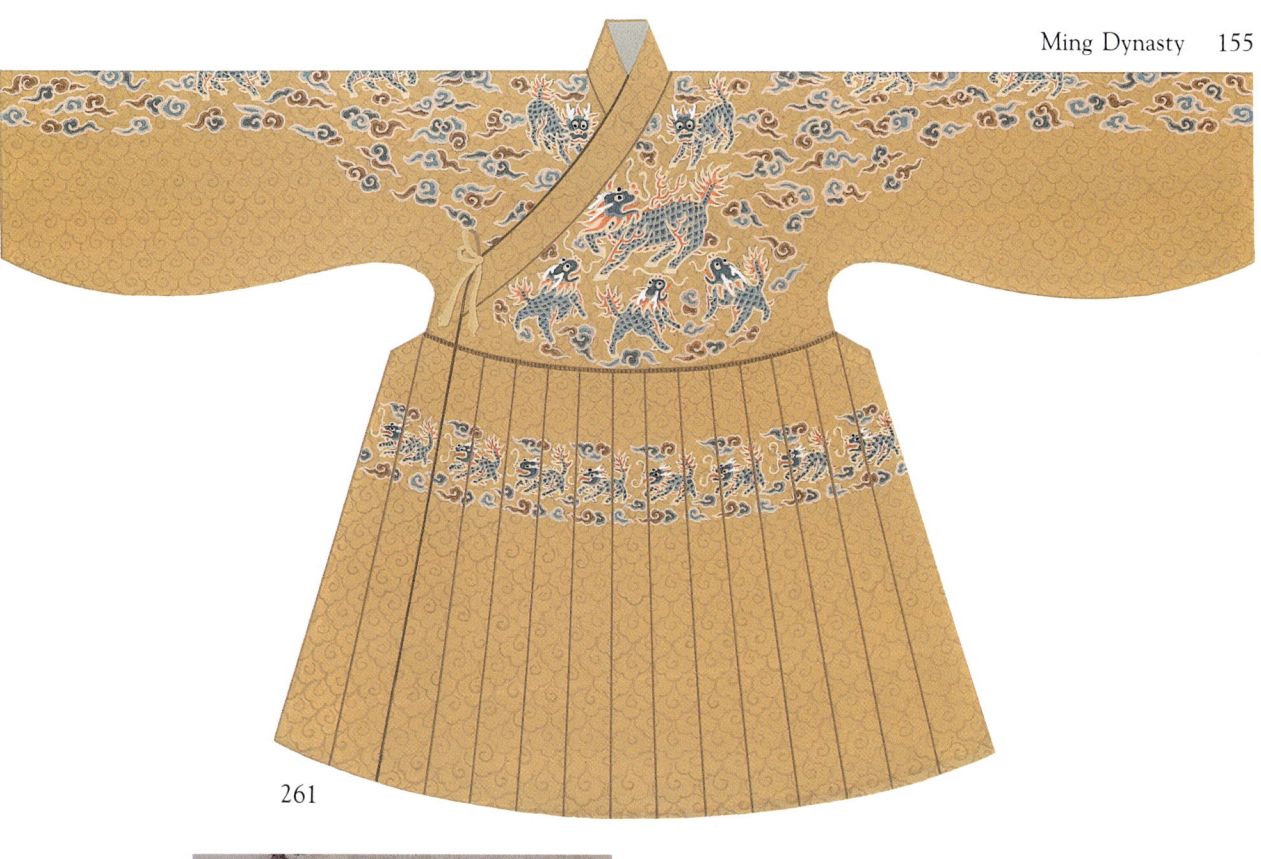

Ming Dynasty 155

261

262

264

263

265

156 Ming Dynasty

266

4. Ordinary Dress for Noblemen

The ordinary dress for men in the Ming Dynasty was chiefly the robe, its features being: large lapel, right opening, broad sleeves, and long enough to cover the knees. Materials used for noblemen's ordinary dress were mainly silk and satin, embroidered with patterns. Brocade was also used.

Motifs on the robes invariably symbolized luck and fortune, the most common being circular forms of a Chinese character such as *shou* " 壽 " (long life) surrounded by round clouds and bats, meaning "five bats up holding long life" ("bat" in Chinese is " 蝠 ", pronouced as *fu*, a homonym of " 福 " (good fortune)). This design was particularly popular during the last years of the Ming Dynasty and the early part of the Qing Dynasty, and it was used not only on costumes, but also on household utensils and architectural decorations.

The use of the "baoxiang flower" for adornment on ordinary dress was another trait of men's wear. The baoxiang flower was a symbolic pattern in the shape of a lotus, evergreen plants or peony, but, by means of variations and exaggerations and when threaded with branches and leaves, the pattern was refined into a costume design that was at once graceful and lively. Patterns of this sort were very popular and there are numerous descriptions of them in historical records. They have also been found on items that have been dug up and preserved.

267

Ming Dynasty 157

268

Fig. 266 Broad-sleeved robe (From Songjiang, Shanghai)

Fig. 267 Broad-sleeved robe (From Zhenjiang, Jiangsu Province)

Fig. 268 Broad-sleeved robe (From Zhenjiang, Jiangsu Province)

158 Ming Dynasty

269

270

Fig. 269 Large lapel robe adorned with motifs of "壽" (longevity) upheld by five bats (Drawing based on paintings by Ming artists and extant artifacts)

Fig. 270 A man in quadrangular flat-topped turban and large lapel robe (From "Volume A of Wei Huanchu's Miniatures" by Luo Xubai)

Fig. 271 Robe of knitted satin with *baoxiang* flower and twined branches (Reconstruction based on paintings by Ming artists and extant artifacts)

271

Ming Dynasty 159

272

273

Fig. 272-273 Round-collared upper garment with broad sleeves (From Yangzhou, Jiansu Province)

5. Costumes and Accessories for Scholars

The coronets for scholars were mainly quadrangular flat-topped turban caps, but the black-striped soft turban with strips dangling behind, commonly called the "scholars' turban", was also worn. Dress for scholars, as for officials, was subject to minutely formulated regulations such as "Students wear gowns made of cloth and gauze of jade colour with broad sleeves and black decorative borders. The turbans are of black gauze with hanging strips. Successful candidates in the national civil service examination do not have to change their dress when entering the Imperial Academy". Many such articles have been found in and near Yangzhou and Taizhou, Jiangsu Province; but the colours of the costumes have faded with time to light red and the decorative borders to bluish green, so that they do not agree with accounts given in historical documents. In the Ming Dynasty, this style of dress was called the "straight dress" or "straight body". Many of the scholars in the novel "The Scholars" wore this.

160　Ming Dynasty

Fig. 274　Turban for scholars (From Yangzhou, Jiangsu Province)

Fig. 275　High felt boots (From Yangzhou, Jiangsu Province)

Fig. 276　Square turban (From Yangzhou, Jiangsu Province)

Ming Dynasty 161

6. Jacket and Skirt

Quite a number of women in the Ming Dynasty continued to wear the jacket and skirt. Though decorated with patterns, the skirts were subdued in appearance since light colours were preferred. At the beginning of the reign of Chong Zhen — the last emperor of the Ming Dynasty — skirts were generally pure white in colour; and even when embroidery was used, it was seen only along the hems one or two *cun* (Chinese inch) from the edge of the skirt, serving as a sort of device for weighting the edge. The material was folded into 6 lengths, six widths of material were used for the skirt, hence this poetic line: "The skirt trails its six widths like the waves of the River Xiangjiang". Later, eight widths were used, with dozens of fine pleats collected around the waist so that the skirt moved in ripples with the steps of the wearer. By the end of the Ming Dynasty, the embellishments on the skirt had become more elaborate and refined. The material used was increased to ten widths and the pleats around the waist became even denser, with a different colour for each ruffle. When puffed by breezes, the colours looked like the halo around the moon, hence the name "moonlight skirt". There were also skirts decoratded with large and small irregular stripes or satin embroidered with patterns and gold threads on both edges that were called the "phoenix tail skirt". To crown it all, there was the "hundred-ruffle pleated skirt", which was made of a single piece of satin material.

Fig. 277 Jacket and skirt (Reconstruction based on paintings by Ming artists portraying beautiful women

Fig. 278 Women musicians in jackets and skirts (Painting)

162   Ming Dynasty

279

280

Fig. 279   Jacket and skirt with waist skirt (Reconstruction based on paintings by Ming and Qing artists, portraying beautiful women)

Fig. 280   Atendant maids in jackets and skirts (From "Fine Works Portraying Beautiful Women by Fei Xiaolou)

Fig. 281   A jacket (Now in Zhenjiang Museum, Jiangsu Province)

Fig. 282   A skirt (Now in Zhenjiang Museum, Jiangsu Province)

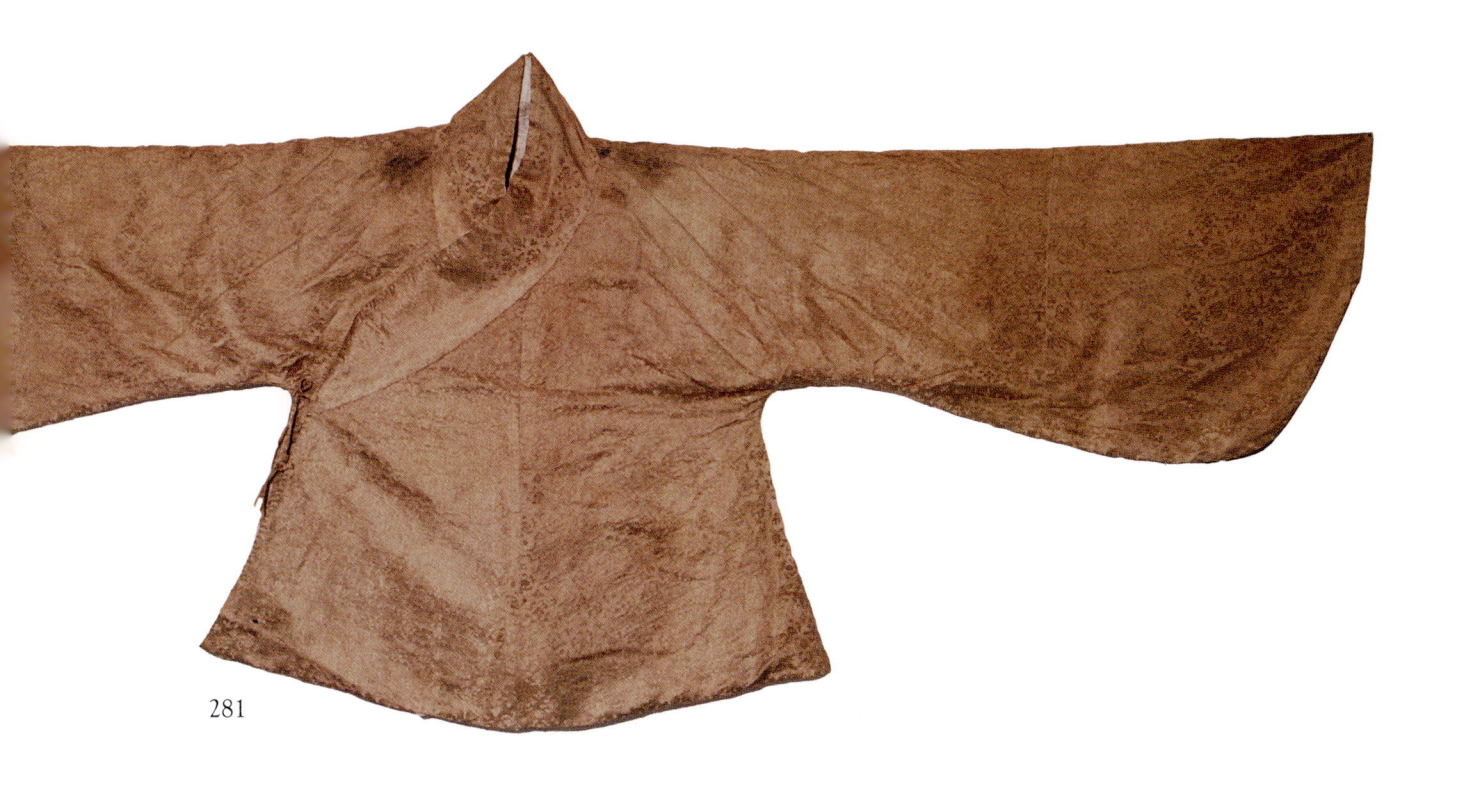

Ming Dynasty 163

281

282

164 Ming Dynasty

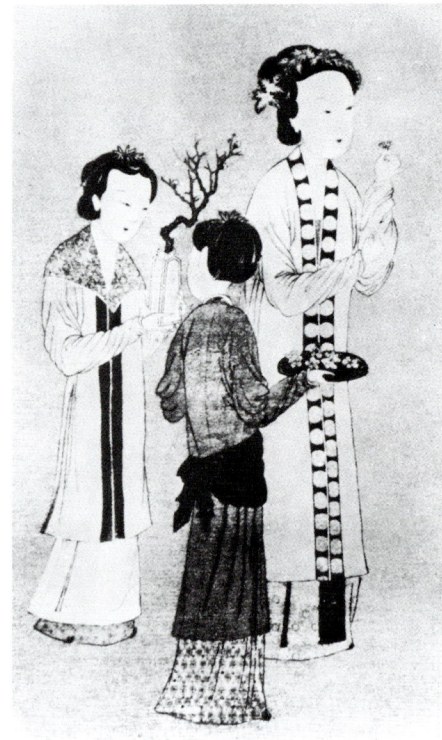

283

7. Over-dress and Sleeveless Over-dress

The over-dress was also often worn by women of the Ming Dynasty. Its basic style was similar to that of the Song Dynasty, with front opening and reaching below the knees. By the end of Ming and beginning of Qing, modifications were made to widen the sleeves and lower the collar, as reflected in the Qing painting "Screen Picture of the Revels of the Imperial concubine".

The sleeveless over-dress was a kind of riding jacket with front opening, said to have originated in the Yuan Dynasty, when it was first worn by the emperor and later became popular among commoners. Still later it became a kind of women's costume and by the middle of the Ming Dynasty, it had become a favourite dress for ladies, particularly for young women. It remained very popular even in the Qing Dynasty, and the riding jacket (or vest) that appeared later evolved from this kind of over-dress.

284

Fig. 283 A noblewoman and attendant maids in narrow-sleeved over-dress ("Lady with Pinned Flowers" by Tang Yin)

Fig. 284 Narrow-sleeved over-dress (Reconstruction based on paintings of beautiful women by Ming artists)

Ming Dynasty 165

Fig. 285 Broad-sleeved over-dress (Reconstruction based on paintings of beautiful women by Ming and Qing artists)

Fig. 286 A noblewoman in broad-sleeved over-dress ("Screen Picture of the Revels of the Imperial Concubine", by a Qing artist)

166 Ming Dynasty

287

Fig. 287 A woman wearing sleeveless over-dress (From the picture album "Leisurely Repose")

Fig. 288 Sleeveless over-dress (Reconstruction based on paintings of beautiful women by Ming artists)

288

Ming Dynasty

290

8. Paddy-field Design Dress

The paddy-field design dress was a costume made from colourful fragments of satin materials pieced and stitched together, looking like the patchwork outer vestment worn by a Buddhist monk. The dress was called *shui tian yi* (paddy-field dress) because its criss-cross patterns resembled those of a paddy field. Simple, and unique, yet producing a special ornamental effect, it won great popularity among women during the Ming and Qing Dynasties. It is said that as early as in the Tang Dynasty, people began to make clothes using this patching method, as described in a line from a poem by the Tang poet Wang Wei: "Learn the art of tailoring by following the patterns of the paddy fields". At first much attention was paid to proportion so that all the selected satin materials had to be cut into rectangular strips before being systematically arranged and sewn into a garment; but as time went by, the prescribed patterns were less and less rigidly adhered to, and the strips could be of different sizes and shapes so that the finished garment looked very much like a stage costume called *bai na yi* (much-patched garment) or *fu gui yi* (rich costume).

Fig. 289 Dress style of paddy-field design garment (Reconstruction based on paintings of beautiful women by Ming and Qing artists)

Fig. 290 A woman in paddy-field design dress (From the picture album "Leisurely Repose")

168　Ming Dynasty

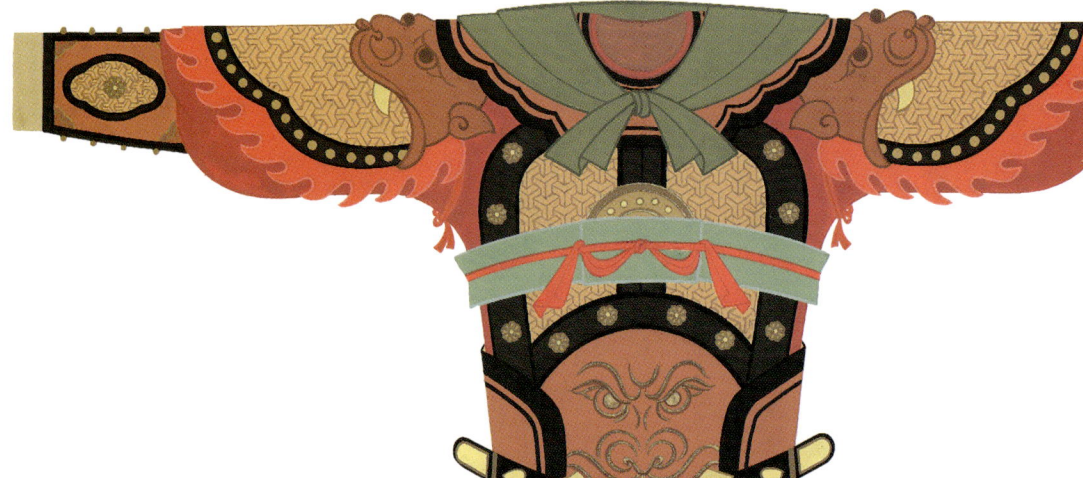

9. Armour

One of the costumes for military personnel in the Ming Dynasty was the "fat coat", for which the regulations were that it should be long enough to reach the knees, have narrow sleeves, and be padded with cotton. As the colour of the costume was red, it was also called the "red fat coat". Cavalrymen often wore this kind of coat with front opening to facilitate riding. In battle, combatants also wore helmets which were often made of steel and seldom of leather. Armour worn by commanding officers was made of copper or iron, with the protective plates formed in the shape of the Chinese character "山" (mountain). The armour was of excellent workmanship and convenient to wear. The rank and file wore the "interlocked iron armour" and below the waistline the skirt and trousers were made of iron wire, which was also used in making combat boots.

Fig. 291　Dress style of suit of armour worn by commanding officers (Reconstruction based on stone carvings and paintings)

Ming Dynasty 169

292

293

Fig. 292 A military officer in full armour (Stone carving in Ding Ling, Beijing)

Fig. 293 Helmet (From Ding Ling, Beijing)

Fig. 294 Warrior in full armour (Pottery figurine)

294

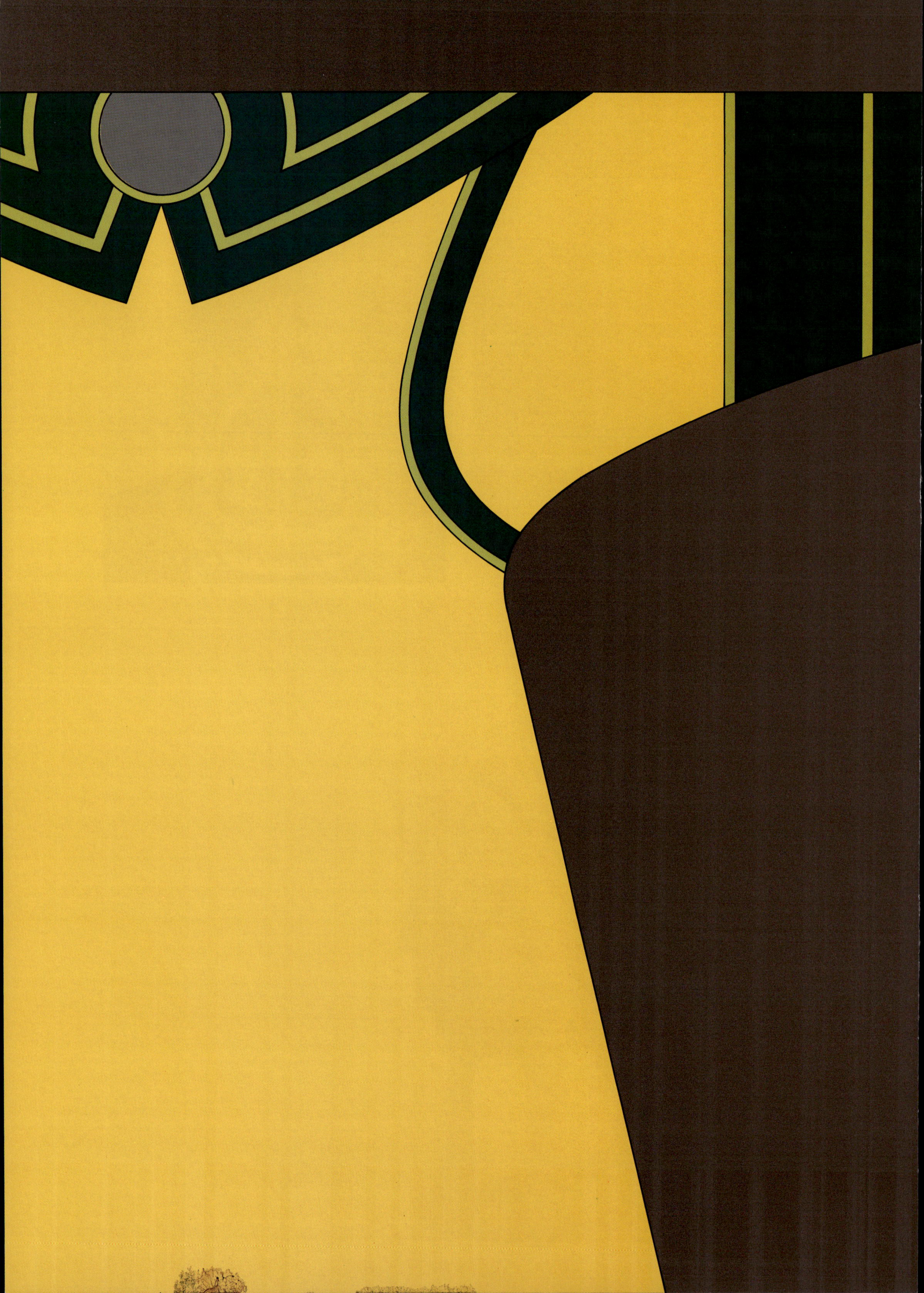

清

QING DYNASTY

After the Manchu dynasty of Qing conquered China, they compelled the Han people to observe their customs by imitating the Manchu ways of dress. In the whole history of the evolution of dress, it can be seen that the dress system of the Qing Dynasty was the most complicated and multifarious. As the dynasty was not too far removed from the present age, a considerable number of articles of clothing belonging to that period are still in existence.

As a rule, men of the Qing Dynasty shaved part of their hair and plaited the rest into a queue. Their headgear can be classified into the ceremonial hat and the cap for casual wear. The ceremonial or official hat, commonly called the "Big Hat", consists of two kinds: the "warm hat" worn in winter and the "cool hat" used in summer. According to the rule, people did not begin wearing the summer hat until the third month of the year. With the coming of the eighth month, they replaced it with the winter hat. The winter hat, mostly round in shape, had a brim round it and was made of leather in most cases, though some were made of silk, wool or cotton cloth, all depending on the weather in which the hat was to be worn. From the centre of the crown of the winter hat spread out like radii a number of red silk braids, popularly called the "red tassels", surmounted by a pearl, the colour — red, blue, white or golden — of which depended on the rank of the wearer. The summer hat was of a conical shape, made of rattan, bamboo, thin bamboo strips or wheat stalks wrapped in silk. It was mostly white, but there were also light green and yellow hats. Like the winter hat, it had a red tassel and a pearl on top. The two above-mentioned formal hats must be equipped with a tube two inches long fixed somewhere below the pearl to hold the feather, which, in turn, was of two kinds: the coloured feather and the blue feather. The former was made of peacock's feather and the latter of pheasant's feather. They were used to show the rank of the user. The peacock feather was again classified into three grades: "one eye" (meaning one feather), "two eyes" (meaning two feathers) and "three eyes" (meaning three feathers). The last represented the most elevated rank and was only fit for the son of a Manchu prince of royal blood.

The cap, worn by officials and the common people alike, was also known as the "small cap". So many were its styles that they varied with the circumstances in which the cap was worn. The commonest kind was the skullcap, which resembled half a watermelon. Its make and use were the same as the hexagonal cap of the Ming Dynasty. Skullcaps for summer and autumn wear were made of thin gauze, while those for spring and winter wear were made of satin. In general, the colour of the skullcap was black and its lining red. At the top of the cap was a knot made of red silk thread, which was replaced by a black or white one when people were in mourning. During winter, people generally wore a cowl-like hat, chiefly made of silk or wool and stuffed with cotton inside. The red ones were worn by people of exalted position.

Men's dress consisted of robes, gowns, jackets, upper garments and trousers. Robes and gowns formed the most essential part of the ceremonial costume. The robe of the Qing Dynasty had slits: two slits for officials and scholars, and four for the imperial family. The robe without slits was called "Wrapped Round the Body", and was to be worn by commoners. The robe with slits was equipped with cuffs specially made to suit the need of a mounted archer. As the cuff took the form of a horseshoe the sleeve was called "Horse-shoe sleeve". Ordinarily, the cuff was turned up, but the wearer turned it down when saluting. Even the designs on the robe were strictly prescribed: dragons for the imperial couple, and pythons for noblemen. Gowns were generally worn as outer garments, hence the name "outer gowns". To suit different seasons, they might be unlined, lined, padded with cotton or lined with fur. But the use of transparent gauze and sheepskin as a dress material was forbidden, because gauze revealed the skin underneath, while clothes lined with sheepskin were too much akin to mourning apparel. The Qing mandarins' outer garments were mostly dyed azurite — a reddish black colour. In addition, in the middle of both the front and the back part was a patch of cloth. The garment was therefore called "patched gown" or "patched clothes". The patches, following the Ming dress system, were usually embroidered with the forms of animals: birds for civil officials and animals for military officers. There was another kind of outer garment that reached only to the waist. It was at first part of the army uniform under the name of *ma gua* or riding jacket simply because it suited the rider very well. Later, it became the general wear irrespective of sex or rank and finally came to be a form of ceremonial costume. Lastly, there was the vest worn by either men of women.

The Qing women's hairstyle consisted of two types: the Manchu and the Han styles, each strictly adhering to its own national tradition at first, but gradually interacting to form new varieties.

In the middle of the Qing Dynasty, the hairstyle of the Han women chiefly took after the fashion of the Manchu maid of honour and the "high-rising coil" became popular. The hair combed into two parts was given the popular name of "fork-shape hair". There was also a tress of hair hanging down behind, with its end trimmed into the shape of a tail called the "swallow's tail". Later styles that came into fashion were the flat bun, the round bun and the *ru yi* ("after one's heart") bun. At the close of the dynasty, braids became very much the vogue, at first among young girls, but gradually growing in popularity till they formed the chief hair style of middle-aged as well as young women.

Besides hair clasps and hairpins, the Han women's headdress included a variety of other ornaments. Elderly women usually wore at the back of the head a "coronet" made of cardboard the purpose of which was to preserve the shape of the hair. Those who wore no "coronet" covered their bun with a black net. Most middle-aged women liked to wear a *zuan,* which was shaped like a bowl and was usually made of palm-fibre, or hemp and covered in silk embroidered with gold or silver flowers. A woman also wore above her brow a headpiece made of a piece of silk and embroidered with auspicious designs. It was worn in autumn and winter by women of rank as a kind of ornament and by their poorer counterparts to resist the cold.

Manchu women of position generally decorated their hair with a small comb whose frame was formed with wire or thin rattan strips and covered with black gauze, on which were embroidered green feathers. The commoners mostly wore "fork-shape" buns. Later, under the influence of the Han women, they came to wear flat buns. However, the bun became higher and higher towards the end of the dynasty until it was an ornament of fixed shape in the form of an "archway", capable of being put on the head at will after putting a few flowers into it, hence the name of "big wings".

The dress of the Han women underwent smaller changes than that of men after the establishment Manchu rule, on the principle that "men, not women, follow" (meaning that the Han men, rather than women, should strictly follow the Manchu dress regulations).

In accordance with the Ming tradition, empresses, imperial concubines and ladies of rank continued to wear the "phoenix coronet" and the "rosy scarf" as official costume, while commoners could only wear cloak, jacket and skirt. The cloak was the outer garment for Qing women. Its function was the same as that of a man's gown. It had roomy sleeves, and reached to the knees, with its front parted in the middle and buttoned all the way down. The cloak had a low collar decorated with jewellery and under it were an outer and an inner blouse. The latter was a sort of underwear in various shades of red, pink, peach, or pink. The ordinary wear for Manchu women was the long gown, whose shape was similar to that of a man's gown and also having embroidered collar and cuffs.

Women, in general, wore skirts as their lower garments, and red skirts were for women of position. At first, there were still the "phoenix-tail" skirt and the "moonlight" skirt and others from the Ming tradition. However the styles evolved with the passage of time: some skirts were adorned with ribbons that floated in the air when one walked; some had little bells fastened under them: others had their lower edge embroidered with wavy designs. As the dynasty drew to an end, the wearing of trousers became the fashion among commoners women. There were trousers with full crotches and over-trousers, both made of silk embroidered with patterns.

According to the Qing regulations civil officials of the fifth rank and military officers of the fourth rank (including titled ladies) should wear ceremonial pearls along with the official costume. The masculine part of the populace, too, observed the custom of hanging ornaments about their persons. They had a variety hanging from the waistband. There were for example, various kinds of wallets with different shapes, declarations and names, such as "chicken's heart", "gourd", etc. In addition, there were also purses, fan-bags, perfume-satchels, knives, spectacle-cases and other items. Women, on the other hand, carried only a few trifles in the way of ornaments, such as ear-picks, tooth-picks, and hair tweezers, attached to the front part of their garments.

The men of the Qing Dynasty wore shoes to match their ordinary clothes, but they changed into boots when wearing their official costume. Boots were chiefly made of black satin. The square toes which had been popular in the beginning were later replaced by pointed toes, although court etiquette still prescribed the wearing of square-toe boots. There were also *ya feng* boots worn by high-ranking officials and the light *pa shan hu* boots worn by military officers and officers of the law. The multiplicity of the shapes of shoes can be attested by the following terms: "the cloud-patterned toe", "the flat toe", "the inlaid", "the double-ridge", and the "single-ridge". It was very common for the women of the Qing Dynasty to bind their feet. The Han women, in general, wore bow-shaped shoes. The Manchu women, however, did not bind their feet and mostly wore embroidered shoes with raised wooden underpart.

The armour of the Qing officer was generally made of silk decorated with studs, while the common soldiers wore numbered uniforms when they went to war.

1. Emperor's Costume and Accessories

The court crown for the emperor was made of marten or black fox fur in winter, and of perfectly white straw or thin vine and bamboo strings in summer. A red tassel was always attached to the crown. The court robe was bright yellow, but when offering sacrifices to Heaven, the Sun, and the Moon, the emperor wore blue, red or white respectively. The robe was embroidered with dragons — two for the shoulders, five for the waist, one on the lapel, nine each on the front and back of the folds. On the skirt there were two rampant dragons and four running dragons. On the shawl there were two running dragons, and at the cuff of each sleeve there was one rampant dragon. To set these off there were twelve decorative designs. The dragon robe was also bright yellow, though gold or orange were also used. For background there were twelve decorative designs, spaced with cloud patterns in five colours.

According to Qing court etiquette, the emperor's dragon robe fell into the category of costumes for festive occasions. Slightly less imposing than the court and sacrificial robes, it was nevertheless the most frequently worn. When wearing the dragon robe, the monarch must also wear a special hat and girdle as well as a necklace to complete the attire.

In ancient days, the term "*jiu wu zhi zun*" (loftiness of nine and five) was synonymous with the throne. The numbers nine and five usually symbolized majesty and were given expression not only in palace architecture but also in the everyday utensils of the imperial household. According to historical documents, the Qing emperor's dragon robe was also decorated with nine dragons, but pictures and real objects invariably reveal only eight, leaving the viewer puzzled as to where the ninth dragon could be. Some say that the emperor himself should naturally be counted in as one. In fact the ninth dragon was embroidered on the reverse side of the lapel and was therefore not easily seen. However, when viewed from front or back alone. Only five dragons were visible (the dragons over the shoulders being visible from both front and back). In this sense, nine did "coincide" with five.

The lower part of the dragon robe was ornamented with numerous curvy lines called *shui jiao* (water foundation), above

Fig. 295 Emperor's court robe (Painted according to an actual robe)

Qing Dynasty 175

Fig. 296 An emperor wearing court crown and court robe (From "Portraits of Emperors and Empresses" in Palace Museum, Beijing)

Fig. 297 Court boots (Now in Palace Museum, Beijing)

176 Qing Dynasty

which were patterns representing surging waves, and over the waves were designs of mountains, rocks and treasures. All these were not only auspicious implications of a lasting reign. But also symbols of the permanent unity and prosperity of the empire.

Fig. 298 Dragon robe — front view (Drawing of an actual robe)

Qing Dynasty 177

Fig. 299 Dragon robe — rear view (Drawing after an actual relic)

2. Empress' Costume and Accessories

The empress' costume consisted of the court hat, jacket, robe, skirt, and, for festive occasions, the dragon jacket and dragon robe.

The court hat was made of marten fur for winter and green wool for summer and both styles were adorned with fringes. The top of the bonnet had three layers, each decorated with Sungari pearls, on top of which stood golden phoenixes inlaid with precious stones. To protect the collar there were two bright yellow stripes at the back of the hat, which were also inlaid with jewels.

The court jacket had three styles, each azurite in colour and decorated with gold patterned edges (a kind of gold brocade border). The patterns were of dragon: some in a stately posture, others flying. For two of the three styles, the middle part was pleated. The hems were decorated with running dragons or colourful waves and patterns standing for endless happiness and longevity. Court robes were of five kinds. They were all of bright yellow satin, embroidered with dragons, and were hung with such ornaments as gold bracelets, necklaces, earrings, pearl necklaces and scented handkerchiefs. While men (the emperor included) wore only one string of pearls around the neck, the empress and titled ladies wore three.

Fig. 300 Court Hat (Actual relic, now in Palace Museum, Beijing)

Fig. 301 An empress in court hat and robe (From "Portraits of Emperors and Empresses of the Qing Dynasty", in Palace Museum, Beijing)

Qing Dynasty 179

Fig. 302 Court costume (Drawing based on actual relic)

Fig. 303 Court over-jacket (Actual relic, now in Palace Museum, Beijing)

180 Qing Dynasty

304

305

Qing Dynasty 181

306

Fig. 304   Empress' ordinary dress — "phoenix garment" (Drawing based on picture of actual relic)

Fig. 305   Empress' ordinary dress — "hundred-butterfly garment" (Drawing based on picture of actual relic)

Fig. 306   An empress dowager in ordinary dress (Actual portrait)

Fig. 307   High sole shoes (Now in Palace Museum, Beijing)

307

3. Costume and Accessories for Officials

Costume and adornment for ranked civil and military officers including the court hat, the hat and costume for festive occasions, the robe with embroidered square patch at mid-front and back, the court robe and the python robe. Rank was distinguished by the jewel on the top of the hat, and the design of the patched garment and python robe. The jewels were as follows: ruby for the 1st rank, coral for the 2nd, sapphire for the 3rd. Lapis lazuli for the 4th, crystal for the 5th, tridacna shell for the 6th, gold for the 7th, gold top with incised inscriptions for the 8th, and gold top with Chinese characters cut in relief for the 9th. Those without jewels on their hats were non-ranked officials and officers. The ornaments worn on hats for festive occasions were about the same as those for the court hats, but at the back of the former there were quills of different colours for different ranks. Specifically, officials and officers of 6th rank or under used blue quills, while those of 5th rank or above used peacock quills. The python robes could be blue or azurite in colour. For 1st to 3rd rank the robe was embroidered with nine five-clawed pythons; for 4th to 6th, eight four-clawed pythons; and for 7th to 9th, five four-clawed pythons. From princes down, all ranked personages wore azurite-coloured robes with embroidered square patches. For civil officials the patches were embroidered with birds, while for military officers they were embroidered with animals. As far as shape was concerned, patches for relatives of the emperor were either round or square. The embroidered birds were as follows: a crane for the 1st rank, golden pheasant for the 2nd, peacock for the 3rd, wild goose for the 4th, lophura for the 5th, egret for the 6th, violet mandarin ducks for the 7th, quail for the 8th and long-tailed flycatch for the 9th. With regard to the kinds of embroidered animals for military officers, *qi ling* (Chinese unicorn) was for the 1st rank, lion for the 2nd, leopard for the 3rd, tiger for the 4th, bear for the 5th, young tiger for the 6th, rhinoceros for the 7th and 8th, and sea horse for the 9th. All civil officials of 5th rank upwards and military officers of 4th rank upwards, as well as judicial officials and high-ranking imperial bodyguards, were also required to wear necklaces consisting of 108

Qing Dynasty 183

309

beads threaded together. Each necklace had 3 strings of smaller bead necklaces attached to it. For men there were two strings on the left, and for women the same number on the right. There was yet another string of beads called *bei yun* (or "back cloud"), which hung down the wearer's back.

Fig. 308 Court robe embroidered with pythons (Actual robe)

Fig. 309 Plain court robe with golden borders — rear view (Actual robe)

Fig. 310 Over-collar (Actual item)

184   Qing Dynasty

Fig. 311   Summer hat (Actual item)

Fig. 312   Winter hat (Actual item)

Fig. 313   Hollow stems of quills (Actual item)

Fig. 314   Robe with round patches of coiled dragons (Actual robe)

Fig. 315   One of emperor's close relatives in winter hat and robe with round embroidered patches, wearing a necklace (Actual portrait)

Fig. 316   Jewels for ornamenting top of hats (Actual item)

Fig. 317   A necklace (Actual item)

Qing Dynasty 185

314

315

316  317

Fig. 318 Embroidered patch for 1st rank civil official — crane

Fig. 319 Embroidered patch for 2nd rank civil official — golden pheasant

Fig. 320 Embroidered patch for 3rd rank civil official — peacock

321

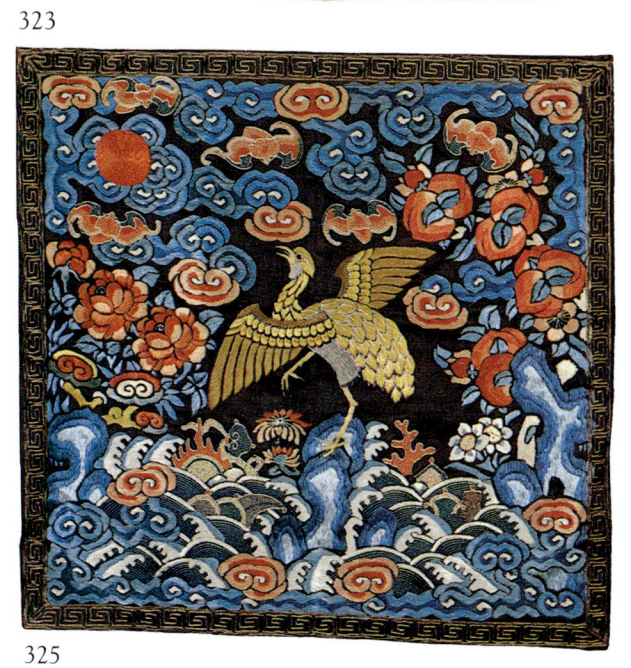

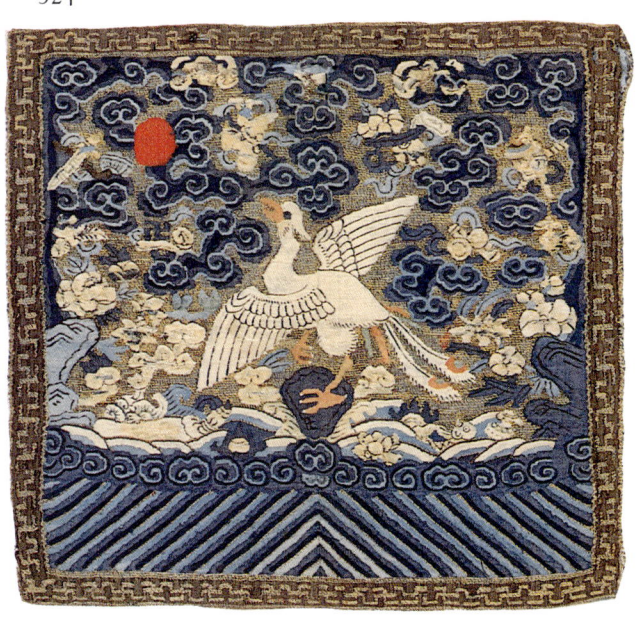

322

323

324

325

326

188 Qing Dynasty

327

328

329

330

331

Fig. 321   Embroidered patch for 4th rank civil official — wild goose

Fig. 322   Embroidered patch for 5th rank civil official — lophura

Fig. 323   Embroidered patch for 6th rank civil official — egret

Fig. 324   Embroidered patch for 7th rank civil official — violet mandarin duck

Qing Dynasty 189

332

Fig. 325 Embroidered patch for 8th rank civil official — quail

Fig. 326 Embroidered patch for 9th rank civil official — long-tailed flycatcher

Fig. 327 Embroidered patch for a prince — coiled dragon

Fig. 328 Embroidered patch for 4th rank military officer — tiger

Fig. 329 Embroidered patch for 3rd rank military officer — leopard

Fig. 330 A civil official in robe with embroidered square patch (Actual portrait)

Fig. 331 A Qing Dynasty military officer in robe with embroidered patch ("Portrait of General Guan Tianpei" by a Qing artist)

Fig. 332 Python robe (Actual robe)

Fig. 333 An official in python robe (Actual portrait)

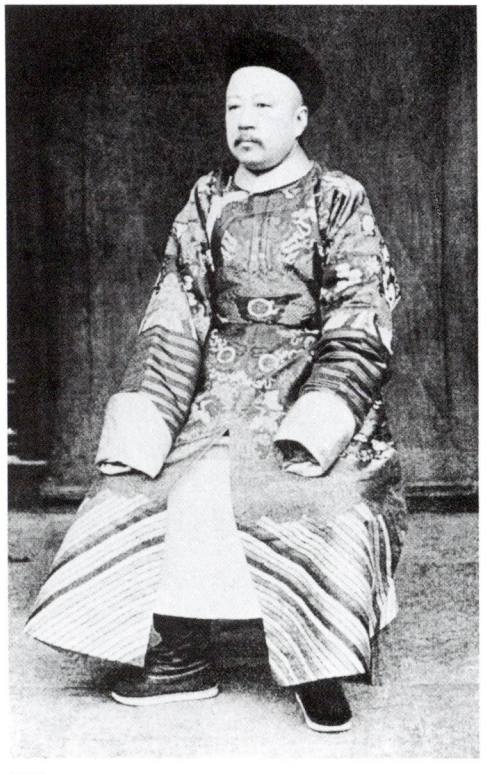

333

Fig. 334 Python robe (Actual robe)

4. Men's Ordinary Wear

The robe was men's chief ordinary wear in the Qing Dynasty. Sometimes for convenience when riding the part that should have been the right lapel was cut down, replaced by a trimming and then fastened to the robe with buttons. This was called the "lapel-less robe" and was often used as a travelling outfit.

In addition, a short jacket was also worn for travelling. This was so short that it did not even reach the waist and had sleeves barely covering the elbows, so it was used for riding and was therefore called the "riding jacket". In the early years of the Qing Dynasty it was worn by soldiers and used to be called the "victory jacket". But later any civilian, man or woman, was also allowed to wear it in peace time so that it became a kind of casual garment. In the beginning, sky blue was the popular colour, but during the reign of Emperor Qianlong this gave way to a purplish red. Later on, as Prince Fu Wen, one of the most influential personages at court, had a fancy for deep crimson, many people followed suit and this colour was subsequently called *fu* (happy). During the rule of Emperor Jiaqing pinchbeck or light grey became the vogue.

Riding jackets were of different kinds, the highest class being the yellow riding jacket, worn only by special favour of the emperor. With regard to the styles, there were the big lapel jacket, the mid-front opening jacket and the lapel-less jacket. The first kind was usually for casual wear and was worn on top of a robe. The second was for formal occasions while the third, also called the "lute-shaped lapel jacket", was made according to the style of the lapel-less robe and was also used for travelling. As to the quality of the materials, apart from fabrics such as silk and satin, there were also some that were made of skins of wild animals. During the reign of Emperor Qianlong, some people — chiefly prominent officials and aristocrats — wore the jacket inside out. Towards the end of the Qing Dynasty, riding jackets made of seal cloth came into fashion among the gentry and wealthy people, who wore them over a straight-lined robe made of light green spring gauze.

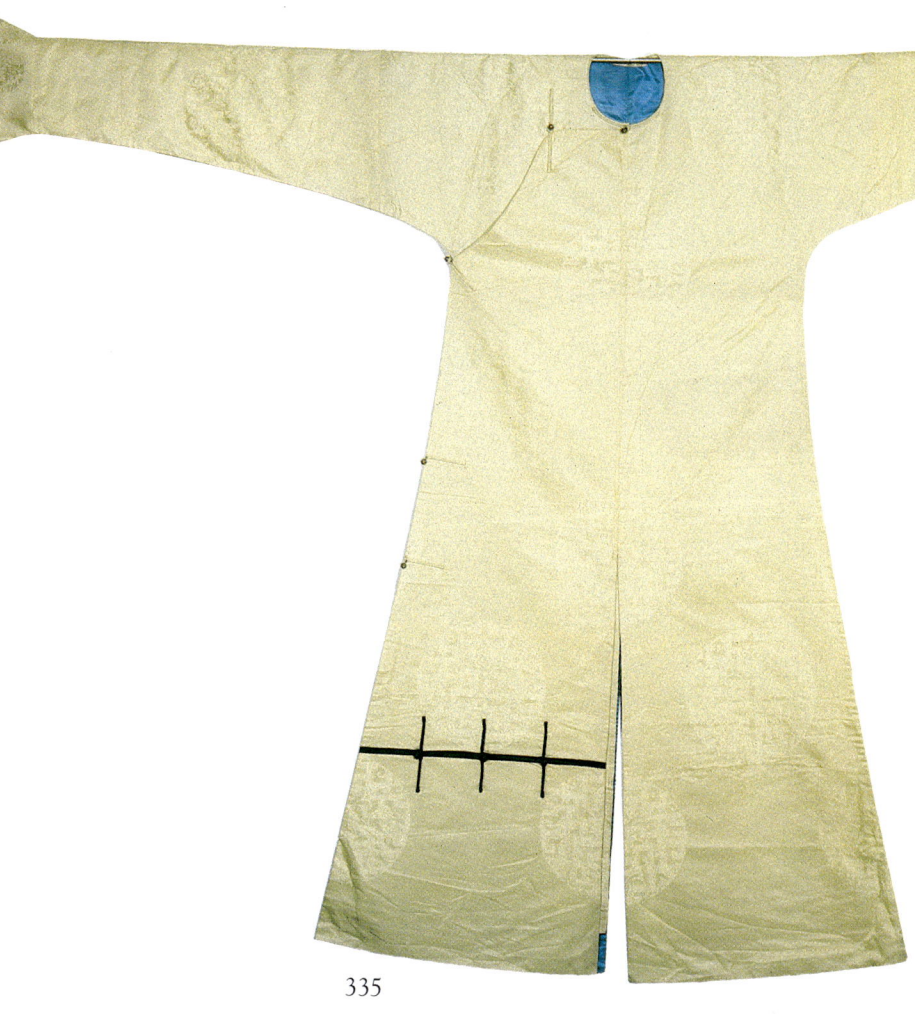

Fig. 335 Robe with lute-shaped — travelling outfit (Actual robe)

Fig. 336 Riding jacket with lute-shaped lapel (Actual robe)

192 Qing Dynasty

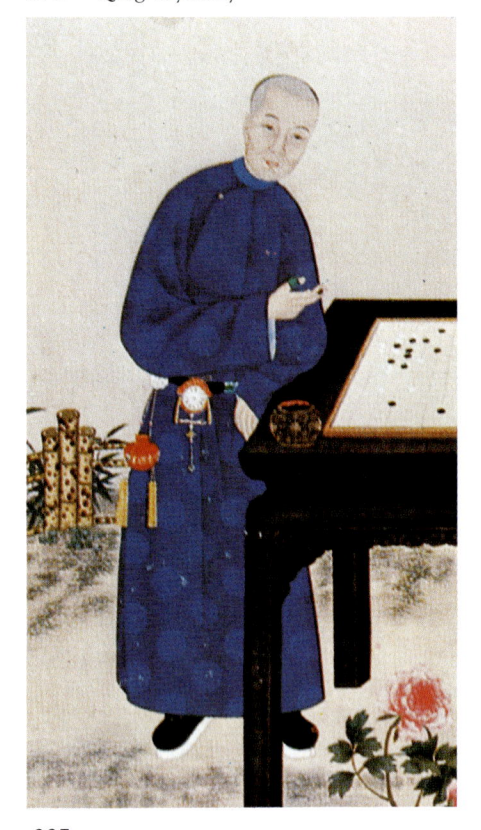

337

338

Fig. 337 A man in ordinary dress and wearing ornaments (Painting preserved in Palace Museum, Beijing)

Fig. 338 An official wearing riding jacket and robe (Actual portrait)

Fig. 339 *Da lian* (pouch worn at the girdle) (Actual item)

Fig. 340 *Da lian* (pouch worn at the girdle) (Actual item)

Fig. 341 Heart-shaped purses (Actual item)

Fig. 342 Cases for folding fans (Actual item)

Qing Dynasty 193

339

341

340

342

194 Qing Dynasty

343

344

5. Ceremonial Dress of Titled Ladies

The ceremonial dress for the empress, the emperor's concubines and other titled ladies in the Qing Dynasty included the phoenix coronet and the sleeveless embroidered cape, their grading being in accordance with the ranks of their husbands.

The sleeveless cape of the Qing Dynasty was slightly different from that of the Ming: the latter was as narrow as a scarf and was without back, while the former was as broad as a vest, with both front and back, and ornamented with an embroidered square badge sewn on both front and back. In addition, the cape was decorated with tassels at the bottom.

345

Fig. 343 A Qing titled lady in phoenix coronet, cloud-patterned scarf and embroidered rosy cape (Actual painting)

Fig. 344 Phoenix coronet (Unearthed relic, now in Zhengjiang Museum, Jiangsu Province)

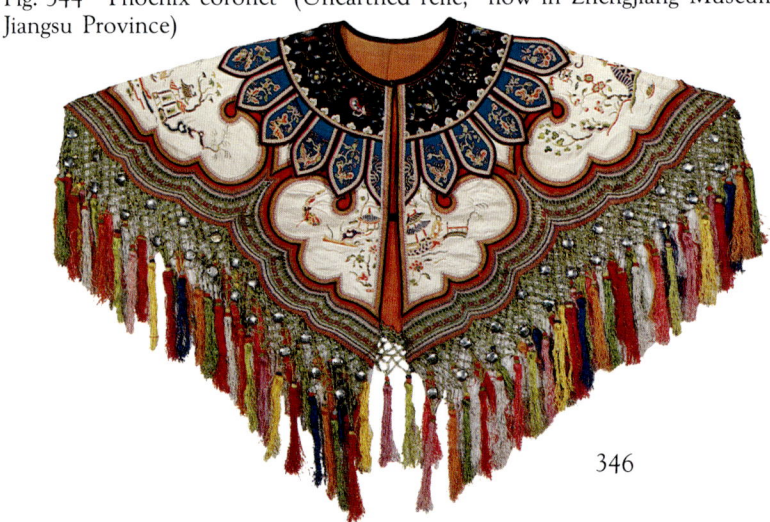

346

Fig. 345 Embroidered rosy cape (Actual cape)

Fig. 346 Cloud-patterned scarf (Actual item)

Fig. 347 Low-collared lined upper garment rimmed with decorative designs (Actual item)

Fig. 348 Pleated horse-face skirt made of purple satin (Actual item)

6. Dresses of Women of Han Nationality

Ordinary women were allowed to wear the phoenix coronet and rosy cape on such rare occasions as weddings and funerals. At other times, however, they could only wear cloaks, lined jackets and skirts as formal dress.

Han women usually wore an overcoat with a hood for going out in winter. The overcoat had evolved from the straw rain cape of the past. At first the cape, under the name of *dou bo* was made from palm fibre and hemp and was worn by men and women against rain or snow; and it was not until Ming and Qing that people began to make silk cloaks, worn not only on wet or snowy days but also in cold weather. After the mid-Qing period, the cloak became the general wear of the womenfolk and its method of manufacture became more complicated. It was mostly made from beautiful silk and printed or embroidered with designs, it was sometimes even lined with fur, and it was very ingeniously tailored; it was also known by the name of "bell" because of its shape.

196 Qing Dynasty

Fig. 349 Embroidered flannelette lined upper garment with buttons down the front (Actual item)

Fig. 350 Narrow-sleeved lined upper garment with decorative borders (Actual item)

Qing Dynasty 197

Fig. 351 Loose-sleeved floral satin lined upper garment with broad decorative borders (Actual item)

Fig. 352 Narrow-sleeved floral satin lined upper garment with broad decorative borders (Actual item)

198 Qing Dynasty

Fig. 353 Embroidered brocade cloak (Actual item)

Qing Dynasty 199

354

7. Costumes of Women of Manchu Nationality

In general Manchu women were in the habit of wearing gowns long enough to cover the shoes. These later developed into the *qi pao*, the dress of the Manchu banner folk. In the beginning the gowns were rather loose and free, but later they became narrower at the waist and then the entire dress was made very slim, thus becoming the characteristic shape of the period. Over the gown there was often a vest, the style of which was similar to the men's waistcoat. The lapel could be tailored into different shapes, the most popular ones being the large, mid-front, lute-shaped, and horizontal line lapels.

Fig. 354 Vest with lute-shaped lapel (Actual item)

Fig. 355 A woman in Manchu hat, long gown and outer vest (Actual portrait)

355

8. Armour

Original nomadic, the Manchu people paid special attention to the skills of riding and archery. The jacket for the Qing warrior, like other jackets then in vogue, also had sleeves in the shape of a horse-shoe. However, with the appearance of guns, artillery, and warships, the drastic changes in modern warfare rendered the traditional armour useless. Although the Qing military officers still wore armour when they were in action, it served no other purpose than that of military insignia and was no protection against modern weapons. Compared with the armour of the Tang and the Song Dynasty, that of the Qing was less significant.

The helmet of the Qing officer, whether made of steel or leather, was covered with a coat of paint. It was decorated with a hawk's feather, an otter's tail or a red flag, in accordance with the rank of the wearer. In general, the armour worn by military officials was made of silk stuffed with cotton. It was also adorned with studs and all sorts of embroidered designs showing the wearer's rank, and had shoulder-plates, armpit-plates and chest-plates, which were attached to the armour with buttons.

356

Fig. 356   Armour for military commanders (Actual item)

Fig. 357   Armour for military commanders — rear view (Actual item)

Fig. 358   A military officer in helmet and armour (Actual photograph)

Fig. 359   Helmet (Actual item)

Qing Dynasty 201

357

358

359

9. Stage Costumes

Stage costumes of the Qing Dynasty in the main followed the system established in the Ming period. According to records, the styles of Qing theatrical dress numbered nearly a hundred, the most common being the *xi zi* (lined coat), *kao* (armour), *pei* (cape), *guan yi* (officials' costume) and *mang* (python robe).

The *xi zi* was the ordinary dress for officials, scholars and common folk, women included. *Kao* was a suit of armour for warriors, especially military commanders. The *pei* was the customary stage costume for the roles of emperor, king, general, high minister, down to lower-ranking officials and gentry. *Guan yi* was a kind of service dress, corresponding to the robe with embroidered square patch of the Ming Dynasty, and confined to ordinary officials. Of all the theatrical costumes, the python robe was the most dignified, its use being confined to the roles of the imperial couple, the emperor's concubines and the close members of the imperial household. The style python robe had round collar, large lapel, embroidered python and dragon on the robe, and patterns of coloured clouds, and sea and river water margins. Below the armpits were attached decorative foils and onto the lower ends of the sleeves long white pieces of fabric were sewn.

360

Fig. 360 Stage costume — python robe (Drawing based on actual item)

Fig. 361-362 Court crown of Prince Zhong — front and profile (Reconstruction based on historical documents and illustrations in the book "Personal Experiences in the Taiping Revolution")

10. Costumes and Accessories of the Taiping Heavenly Kingdom

The Taiping Heavenly Kingdom was the only peasant regime to have a comprehensive system of clothing and accessories. While inheriting the traditional system of past dynasties, the law-makers of the Kingdom set new rules and created new designs to establish a unique system of costume and adornment of their own.

Qing Dynasty 203

regulations for the ensign of each prince and for the colour of uniforms of the rank and file under his command. Specifically, royal guards of the Heavenly King Hong Xiuchuan wore pure yellow military uniforms, while units under the four princes had their yellow uniforms fringed with borders of other colours — green for units of the Eastern Prince, white for those of the Western Prince, red for those under the Southern Prince, and black for those under the Northern Prince. The uniforms were further patched with pieces of yellow cloth at midfront and back, with the characters "太平" (peace) on the front and the characters "聖兵" (holy fighter) or "某軍聖兵"(holy fighter of a certain army unit) on the back. For reserve troops the uniforms were inscribed with the characters "某衙聽使" (at the beck and call of a certain government office).

In ordinary times, the turban was the only headgear for the rank and file of the Taiping Heavenly Kingdom, and only during battles were they allowed to wear helmets, which were mostly made of bamboo, bamboo strips, wicker or rattan and were called *hao mao* (army caps) or *de sheng kui* (victory helmets). On the helmets were colourful patterns of flowers and clouds as well as four white circles inside which were inscribed the four characters "太平天國" (Taiping Heavenly Kingdom).

Caps for generals of the Heavenly Kingdom consisted of the *jiao mao* (angled cap), the *feng mao* (wind cap), the *liang mao* (summer cap) and the *mao e* (visored cap). The *jiao mao* was the court crown with patterns of dragons and phoenixes. The court dress consisted of the robe and the riding jacket. The former was round-collared and loose-sleeved with designs to tell the post and rank of the wearer. The riding jacket was either red or yellow, which, in conjunction with specific designs, also served to identify the wearer's position.

Women's costumes had the following characteristics. In general, the collar was round and the opening was on the left. The sleeves might be either broad or narrow, while the garment usually covered the knees and slits were opened in the middle of the hem and at the sides. Women seldom wore skirts; instead, they preferred wide trousers. The painful costom of foot-binding was abolished at this time.

The later period of the Taiping Heavenly Kingdom saw changes of style in costume as the system of government organization was modified. The costume for Prince Zhong, for instance, was conspicuously different from that of previous princes. His court crown was made of pure gold and on its top there were jewels as well as the designs of a tiger, two phoenixes and a small eagle. His robe was made from yellow satin brocade decorated with twisted threads of three colours — gold, silver and red.

361

362

For instance, in accordance with the joint philosophy of "The School of the Positive and Negative Forces" and "The School of the Five Elements" (metal, wood, water, fire and earth), yellow was designated to represent the central authorities, while blue, red, white and black were to represent east, south, west, and north respectively. Subsequently, four princes were installed to symbolize the four directions, followed by

204 Qing Dynasty

363

364

Qing Dynasty 205

365

366

Fig. 363 Dragon robe of Prince Zhong (Reconstruction based on historical documents and illustrations in the book "Personal Experiences in the Taiping Revolution")

Fig. 364 Prince Zhong in court crown and dragon robe with his generals in hoop-shaped hats and robes (Illustration in the book "Personal Experiences in the Taiping Revolution")

Fig. 365 Riding jacket with coiled dragon designs (Reconstruction based on illustrations in the book "Collection of Facts About the Taiping Rebels")

Fig. 366 Riding jacket with circular floral design (Reconstruction based on illustrations in the book "Illustrated Records of the Quelling of the Long-hair Rebels")

206 Qing Dynasty

367

Fig. 367 Women's narrow-sleeved garment (Reconstruction based on historical documents and illustrations in the book "Personal Experiences in the Taiping Revolution")

Qing Dynasty 207

368

Fig. 368 Women's broad-sleeved garment (Reconstruction based on historical documents and illustrations in the book "Personal Experiences in the Taiping Revolution")

Fig. 369 A women of Taiping Heavenly Kingdom in narrow-sleeved garment with left opening (Selected from illustrations in the book "Personal Experiences in the Taiping Revolution")

369

208 Qing Dynasty

370

371

372

Qing Dynasty 209

373

Fig. 370-371 *Hao mao* (army caps) — front and profile (Reconstruction based on illustrations in the book "Facts About the Taiping Rebels")

Fig. 372-373 Military uniform — front and profile (Reconstruction based on illustrations in the book "Facts About the Taiping Rebels")

374

11. Fabrics and Decorative Borders

The patterns of fabrics used in the Qing Dynasty were mainly adopted from nature. Themes most widely used included a great variety of animals and birds — such as dragons, lions, unicorns, phoenixes and cranes — and flowers and plants — such as plums, orchids, bamboo and chrysanthemums. Other popular designs include *ba bao* (eight treasures) *ba xian* (the eight genii) and the characters "福祿壽", standing for happiness, riches and longevity respectively. The patterns were gorgeous and highly elaborate, and the arrangements were full of variations.

One salient aspect of the costume and accessories of the Qing Dynasty was the extensive use of decorative borders, which has a history of over two millennia. In early times, borders were used solely to increase the life and durability of the garment, and that was why they were fringed on such parts as the collar, lapel, cuffs, and hems, where the garment was subject to wear. Later, however, when the idea arose that the hitherto plain borders could be replaced by decorative ones to create a particular ornamental effect, people began to use embroidery. In time it became such common practice that clothing of all kinds — for men and women and for officials and ordinary people — was fringed with decorative borders. The fashion reached its

375

climax in the reigns of Emperors Xianfeng and Tongzhi, when sometimes practically the entire costume was trimmed with decorations of various sizes, to the extent that the original costume material could hardly be recongnized.

Qing Dynasty 211

377

Fig. 374 An imitation of ancient brocade (Actual item)

Fig. 375 The "hundred sons" brocade (Actual item)

Fig. 376-377 Samples of decorative borders (Tracings of actual items)

376

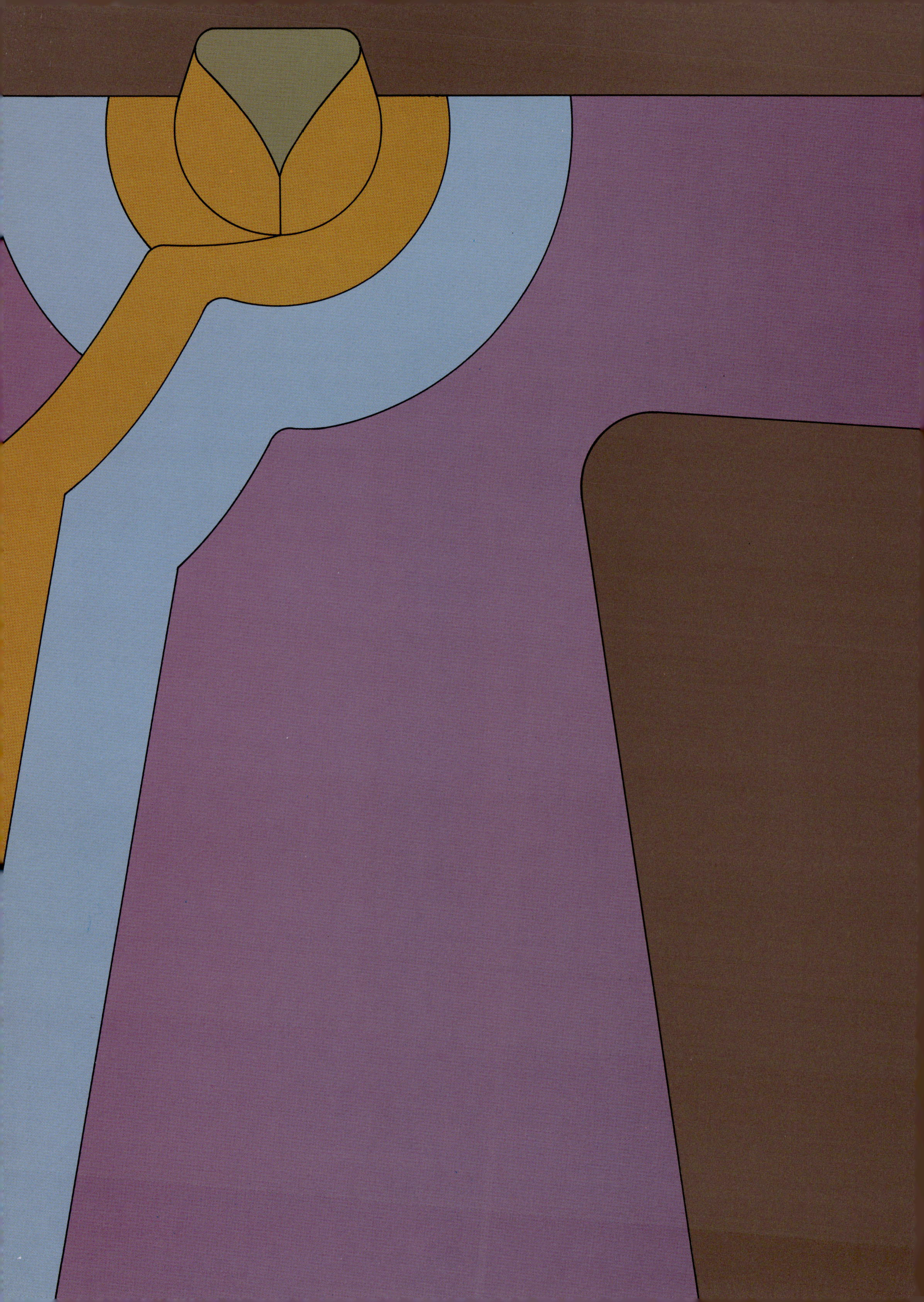

近代

MODERN TIMES

China stepped into the modern era after the Opium War of 1840. Towards the end of the Qing Dynasty, large numbers of Chinese youths went abroad for further studies and were consequently influenced by the progressive thinking of the West. Breaking with the code of feudalism, they cut off their queues and put on western suits. Nevertheless, the costumes of officials and citizens within China remained unchanged, so that when the young students returned from overseas, they had to change back into the traditional costumes of the Qing Dynasty. What's more, they had to wear an artificial queue, or else being condemned or even persecuted.

The Revolution of 1911 overthrew the rule of the Qing Dynasty. Soon after the founding of the Republic, a general order was issued requiring all males to cut off their queues. People of all groups or classes throughout the country complied without delay. At last the custom that had existed for nearly three hundred years was brought to an end. Drastic changes in clothing soon followed. The first major step was to abolish the traditional custom of "identifying one's social status by one's headgear and clothing". Next, the government promulgated costume regulations, calling for the adoption of the dress styles of the western countries. However, as such regulations did not fit in easily with the domestic situation, they were never carried out in full.

At the end of 1920's, the government promulgated new costume regulations, which prescribed ceremonial attire for men and women and uniforms for civil servants, but no specific rules were laid down for ordinary wear. During the 1930's there were no significant changes in men's costumes, though women were showing an increasing interest in their clothes and accessories. Such an interest was further heightened by the influx of foreign clothing materials as a result of the easing of restrictions at ports of entry and exit. And Shanghai, having a relatively developed industry, commerce and culture, and a large population, duly became the centre of women's fashion.

The western trilby was the most formal hat for men in modern times and could be worn on different occasions. There were, in addition, hats such as the skull cap, which underwent many modifications on the basis of its original Qing style. Not only was its pattern renewed, but its material was varied, ranging from otter fur, silk and venetian to satin and palm fibre, chiefly depending on the season. In summer, men usually wore straw hats; and in winter, cowl-like hats or Russian hats. On ordinary days, students wore visored caps, but in summer they wore white, broad-brimmed canvas hats. Labourers and farmers usually wore felt hats in winter, straw hats in summer and bamboo hats on wet days. All the above-mentioned hats were used by wearers in accordance with their identity, social status and profession.

In the early years of the Republic, men's costumes remained basically the same as those worn in the Qing Dynasty. From the 1920's, however, school teachers, clerks and government employees — young ones in particular —in Shanghai and other big cities started to wear western suits, though these were rarely worn by the elderly or by ordinary citizens. The "long gown plus sleeveless outer jacket" remained the major costume for men on formal occasions.

Women's hairstyles varied according to the prevailing mood. Shortly after the founding of the Republic, women, influenced by men's practice of cutting off their queues, also cut their hair short. But this did not last long, and many women soon wore their hair long again. Apart from different forms of buns, young women liked to wear a thin lock of hair over the forehead, called the "bang". The permanent wave, however, was not introduced into China until the early 1930's, when it created a great sensation. Most of the women living in big cities quickly followed the western style and had their hair waved; and some fashion seekers even went so far as to have their hair dyed.

Before the 1920's, women's costumes in general followed the "jacket and skirt" system. Young women often preferred to wear jackets, long and close-fitting with high collars, and full-length black skirt to match. But later, under the influence of the Western way of life, women's costumes became more and more elaborate, and fanciful styles kept coming in. The scholar Jian Shui had this to say when giving a brief account of women's clothing in the twenties: "As regards the dresses, most of them were imported. Hardly had one case of clothing been opened, when it was purchased by anxious buyers, and in a mere three days, imitations could be seen everywhere…. The sleeves were hardly long enough to reach the wrists, but the cuffs measured wider than one foot, and the waist was as slim as a bamboo pole. The garment being collar-less, the wearer's neck looked as long as a crane's. The trouser legs were short but wide, just like those worn by a farmer working in the fields. Through the long silk stockings the human skin was faintly visible… But the costumes are undergoing a new change nowadays: the trouser legs are becoming even wider but long enough to cover the feet, and the upper garment has been shortened to above the waist". Ever since the Tang Dynasty, the design of Chinese women's costumes had kept to the same straight style: flat and straight lines for the chest, shoulders and hips, with few curves visible; and it was not until the 1920's that Chinese women came to appreciate "the beauty of curves", and to pay attention to figure when cutting and making up dresses, instead of adhering to the traditional style.

The most popular item of a Chinese woman's wardrobe in modern times was the *qi pao*. Originally the dress of the Manchus, it was adopted by Han women in the 1920's. Modifications and improvements were then made so that for a time, it became the most fashionable form of dress for women in China.

Two main factors account for women's general preference for the *qi pao:* first, it was economical and covenient to wear. Women of ancient times had to have a complete suit of jacket, trousers, skirt and other articles of clothing for routine wear; now one 'qi pao' would serve the purpose, and it cost much less in terms of material and tailoring, too. Second, it was more fitted and looked more flattering. Since the *qi pao* was a single garment, it outlined a woman's figure to advantage. When matched with high-heeled shoes, which were also very popular at the time, it made the wearer look particularly graceful.

The *qi pao* underwent numerous changes in style after its first appearance, and by the 1930's it had entirely changed from its original form to become unique among women's costumes.

Comparatively speaking, women's costumes and accessories in the 1940's seemed plain; yet they were by no means lacking in style. Apart from the *qi pao,* there were overcoats, western style dresses, vests, woollen sweaters and full-length skirts, complemented or enhanced by scarves, gloves, cameo brooches, ornamental pins, ear-rings, bracelets and rings. A large number of the above-mentioned articles are still in existence.

With regard to footwear, men and women in modern times were seen wearing cloth shoes, leather shoes, sports shoes or sandals. Boots, however, were a rarity south of the Changjiang (Yangtse). From the beginning of the 1920's onwards, high-heeled shoes were the vogue amongst women in large cities.

The traditional armour, which had a history of several thousand years, was completely abandoned in modern times. Men and officers wore uniforms; and cap insignia, collar badges, shoulder badges, chest badges or armbands were used to classify army units and to identify the military ranks.

216 Modern Times

1. Men's Costumes

Influenced by Western culture and life style men of the modern era started wearing western suits. However, a long gown plus vest was still used on formal occasions, co-existing with the western suit.

Men's ceremonial headgear was of two kinds: hats made of black wool fabric for winter, and hats made of white silk cloth for summer. The hat often had a round top and a broad rim. On very formal occasions men wore such hats with both Chinese costume and western suits.

Compared with earlier times, the man's long gown in this period had wider sleeves, but the gown itself was shorter, revealing the trousers below, which could also be either traditional Chinese or western in style. The western-styled trousers had narrower legs with turn-ups; while the traditional Chinese trousers had much wider legs, each tied with a silk band at the bottom, which is how they earned the name "lantern trousers".

Shoes were also of two kinds: traditional and western. The former were made of cloth; while the latter were made of leather, mostly black, though sometimes brown or light brown. Towards the end of the 1920's young students started wearing sports shoes.

Fig. 378 *Ma gua* (ceremonial jacket) with front opening and round patterns (Actual item)

Fig. 379 Flannelette jacquard long gown with patterns of pine and crane (Actual item)

Fig. 380 Western style hat (Actual item)

Fig. 381 A man in western style hat, long gown and *ma gua* (Photograph)

382

384

383

Fig. 382, 384 Hairstyles in the early days of the Republic (Photographs)

2. Women's Hairstyles

From historical records and descriptions in novels, it can be seen that women's hairstyles between the last years of Emperor Guangxu of the Qing Dynasty and the beginning of the Republic chiefly featured the bun. Specifically, there were the spiral bun, the knotted bun, the chain bun, the upward bun, the shoe-shaped "gold ingot" bun, the "musk melon" bun, the one-line bun, the Japanese bun, the "off the horse" bun, the "dancing phoenix" bun, and the "butterfly" bun. In addition, younger women usually had a thin tress of hair, called a bang, covering part of their forehead. The bang, too, was of many styles, with the one-line bang being the first to become popular. This was two Chinese inches long, and generally covered the eyebrows and sometimes even the eyes. Soon the "weeping willow" style came in. The bang was cut into a half circle so that the hair hung like soft willow branches. Later, the bang was parted into two to form angles something like the tail of a swallow and was named the "swallow-tail". In the early days of the Republic, these styles were replaced by an even more popular fashion called the "star-studded sky", to signify something that was not especially noticeable. Around the 12th year of the Republic, women again cut their hair short — sometimes to ear level. In general the hair was then tied up with a silk band. Some women, though, kept their hair in place with a clasp made of pearls, emeralds or other precious stones. In the early 1930's women in China began to have their hair waved.

Fig. 385 Women's hairstyle in 1920's (Photograph)

Fig. 386-387 Women's hairstyles in 1920's (Photographs)

Fig. 388-389 Women's hairstyles in 1930's (Photographs)

220 Modern Times

Fig. 390 The weeping willow bang (Photograph)

Fig. 391 The one-line bang (Photograph)

Fig. 392 The swallow-tail bang (Photograph)

Fig. 393 The "star-studded sky" bun (Photograph)

Modern Times 221

394

395

3. Lined Upper Garment and Skirt

Women's costume in the early 1920's retained the system of jacket and skirt. The upper garment was usually narrow at the waist, its collar was fairly low, and the sleeves only reached to the elbows. The hems were mostly shaped like an arc, while collar, cuffs and front were fringed with decorative borders. The skirt was shortened a little but was still long enough to cover the knees. Some skirts were no longer pleated, so that they hung quite naturally. As for the edges, they were also embroidered with different designs and some were even decorated with colourful jewellery to achieve a sparkling effect.

Fig. 394 Long lined upper garment with high collar and narrow sleeves (Actual item)

Fig. 395 "Horse face" skirt (Actual item)

222　Modern Times

Fig. 396　High-collared red lined silk garment embroidered with silver flower (Actural item)

Fig. 397　High-collared lined garment with embroidered patterns (Actual item)

396

397

Fig. 398　A woman in high-collared long lined garment with narrow sleeves (Photograph)

Fig. 399　Curve-edged short lined garment with broad sleeves (Actual item)

Fig. 400　Embroidered long red skirt (Actual item)

Fig. 401　A woman in curve-edged short lined garment with broad sleeves and embroidered long skirt (Photograph)

398

Modern Times 223

399

401

400

224 Modern Times

Fig. 402 Illustration of lined upper garment and skirt ensemble (Actual item)

Modern Times 225

403

404

Fig. 403 Embroidered satin short lined upper garment edged with pearls (Actual item)

Fig. 404 Embroidered satin short lined upper garment edged with pearls (Actual item)

226 Modern Times

Fig. 405 Embroidered slip-on satin skirt edged with shiny borders (Actual item)

Fig. 406 Embroidered slip-on-satin skirt (Actual item)

Modern Times 227

Fig. 407 Short lined upper garment with front opening and shiny decorative borders (Actual item)

Fig. 408 Lined upper garment and skirt with shiny decorative borders (Actual item)

4. Evolution of *Qi Pao*

Straight, loose and long enough to reach the feet — such were the characteristics of the *qi pao* worn by Manchu women near the end of the Qing Dynasty. It was generally made of silk and satin, and was covered with embroidered patterns. Its collar, cuffs and front were adorned with decorative borders.

The *qi pao* was popular in the early 1920's, but its style showed little difference from the last days of the Qing Dynasty. Soon afterwards, the cuffs were made narrower and the borders were no longer so broad. By the end of the 1920's, its style underwent evident changes owing to the influence of western costumes. For instance, the waist was tightened and the length shortened.

By the 1930's, the *qi pao* had already become the vogue and its style underwent a variety of changes. At first the high collar was much appreciated — the higher the collar, the more fashionable the dress. Even in high summer, when the *qi pao* material looked as thin as the wing of a cicada, a stiff collar high enough to reach the ear was still worn. But gradually the low collar gained favour. When it was quite low, the collarless fashion took over. There were similar changes to the sleeves, now long, so as to cover the wrists, now short, so as to reveal the elbows. The changes in length were even greater. For a time it was made long enough to reach the ground, but later this gave way to a short style that reached only the knees.

The style of the *qi pao* became much simpler in the 1940's. Both gown and sleeves were shortened, and the collar lowered. In summer, it was sometimes made sleeveless and with most of its complicated decorations omitted, so that it accentuated the wearer's figure.

Fig. 409 Embroidered satin *qi pao* with broad decorative borders (Actual item)

Modern Times 229

410

411

412

413

Fig. 410   Manchu costume at end of Qing Dynasty and beginning of the Republic (Photograph)

Fig. 411   A woman in long-sleeved *qi pao* with wavy decorative borders (Photograph)

Fig. 412   A woman in flowered satin *qi pao* with medium-length sleeves (Photograph)

Fig. 413   A woman in check-patterned *qi pao* with medium length sleeves (Photograph)

230　Modern Times

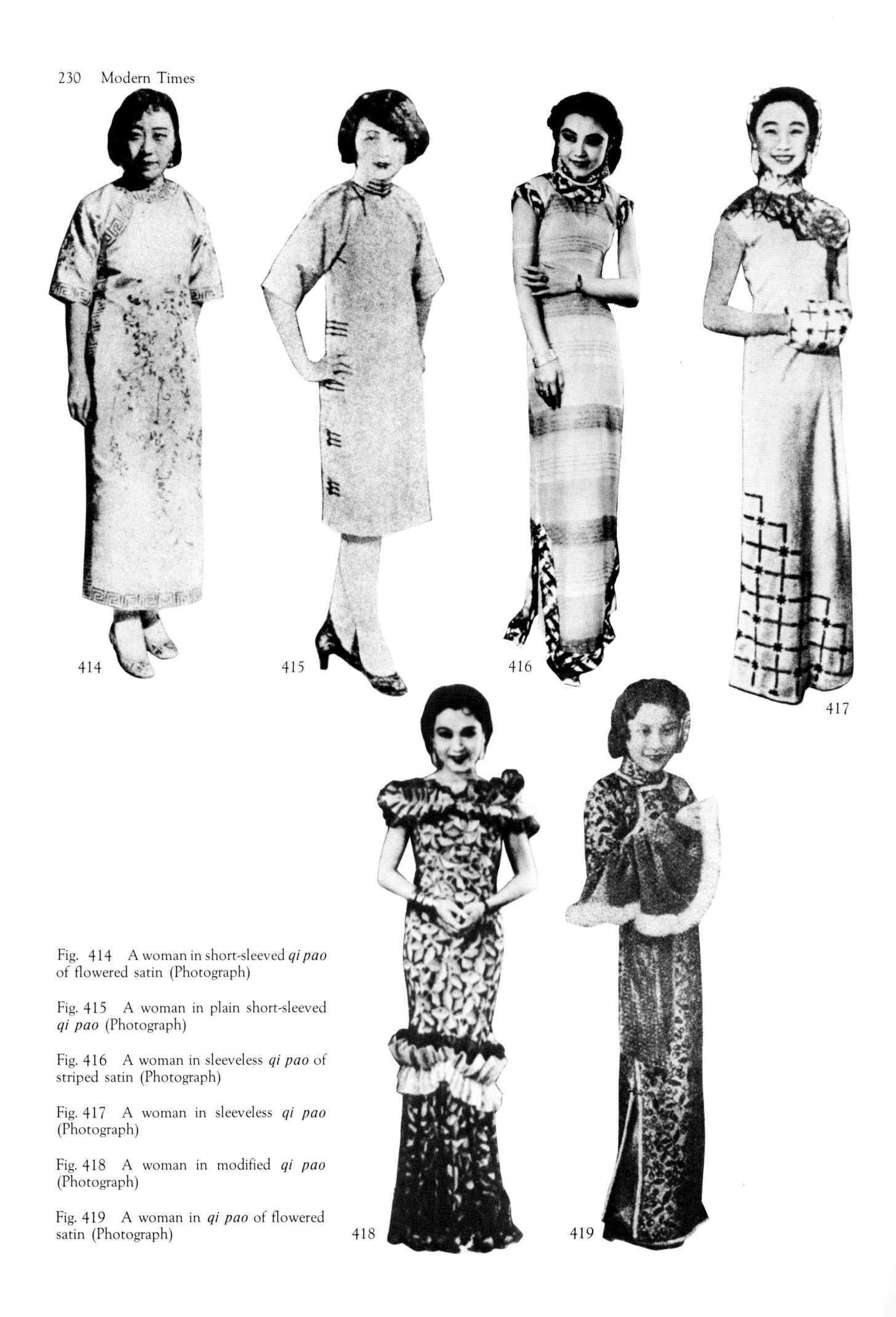

Fig. 414　A woman in short-sleeved *qi pao* of flowered satin (Photograph)

Fig. 415　A woman in plain short-sleeved *qi pao* (Photograph)

Fig. 416　A woman in sleeveless *qi pao* of striped satin (Photograph)

Fig. 417　A woman in sleeveless *qi pao* (Photograph)

Fig. 418　A woman in modified *qi pao* (Photograph)

Fig. 419　A woman in *qi pao* of flowered satin (Photograph)

Modern Times 231

420

421 Fig. 420-421 Embroidered *qi pao* made of flowered stain (Photograph)

232 Modern Times

422

Fig. 422 *Qi pao* with coloured embroidery and broad decorative borders — fashion of Manchu women in Qing Dynasty (Actual item)

Fig. 423 Long-sleeved *qi pao* with side opening and coloured embroidery — fashion in early 1920's (Actual item)

423

Modern Times 233

424

Fig. 424 High-collared *qi pao* with medium-length shoes embroidered with silver cloud-and-dragon patterns — fashion of the mid-1920's (Actual item)

Fig. 425 Long-sleeved *qi pao* with side opening and coloured embroidery — fashion in late 1920's (Actual item)

425

234 Modern Times

426

427

Fig. 426 Close-fitting sleeveless *qi pao* with slit in front — fashion of the early 1930's (Actual item)

Fig. 427 *Qi pao* with shoulder pads, attached sleeves and flowery patterns — fashion of the late 1930's (Actual item)

Fig. 428 Sleeveless tapestry satin *qi pao* with V-shaped opening — fashion in late 1930's (Actual item)

Fig. 429 A woman in short-sleeved, mesh *qi pao* (Photograph)

Fig. 430 Short-sleeved, mesh *qi pao* (Actual item)

Modern Times 235

428

429

430

236 Modern Times

5. Women's Fashions in the 1930's

Though still based on traditional styles, women's costume in the 1930's adopted many features from a wide range of Western fashions to present a unique dress style having a combination of Western and national features.

By this time Shanghai was already the fashion centre in China, leading the styles of women's costume in the country. In 1933, a Shanghai journal published the following rhyme:
Everyone thinks the Shanghai style is fun
It's pretty hard to copy, though;
Before you're even half way done
The next style's in — an endless row.
The rhyme testifies to the rapidity of changes in fashion and the general craze for novel styles of clothing in Shanghai. A comprehensive view of the numerous photographs from this period enables one to sum up the specific features of women's fashions at the time: the *qi pao,* the one-piece Chinese gown, remained the basic costume, yet its collar and sleeves had been westernized. The collar, for instance, was shaped like a lotus leaf, and slits were opened in the sleeves. Matched with a cape or with a woollen sweater over it, the new *qi pao* was graceful and unique.

Fig. 431 A woman in *qi pao* and cape (Photograph)

Fig. 432 A woman in short-sleeved dress with turn-down collar (Photograph)

Fig. 433 A woman in *qi pao* with sleeves shaped like lotus leaves (Photograph)

Fig. 434 A woman in *qi pao* and bow tie (Photograph)

Fig. 435 A woman in Western-style evening dress (Photograph)

Fig. 436 A woman in *qi pao* and short-sleeved jacket (Photograph)

Fig. 437 A woman in short-sleeved dress (Photograph)

Fig. 438 A woman in Western-styled evening dress (Photograph)

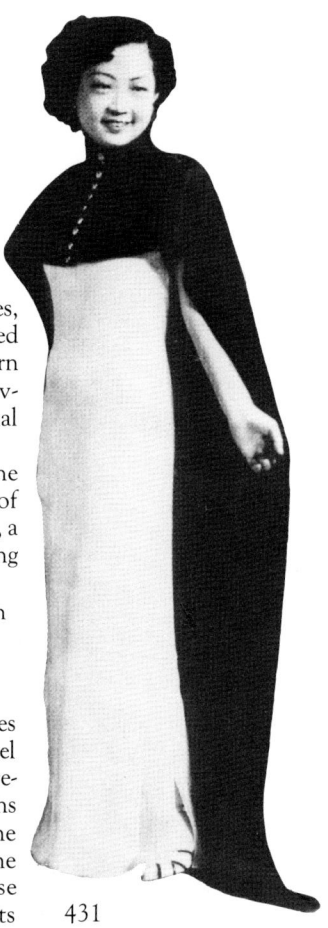

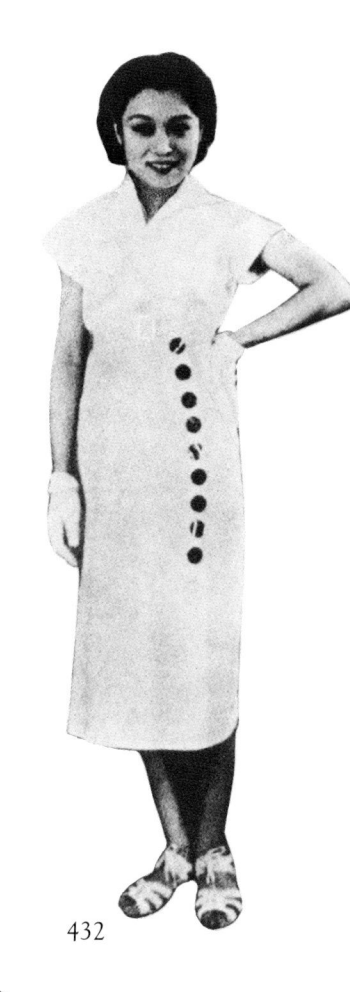

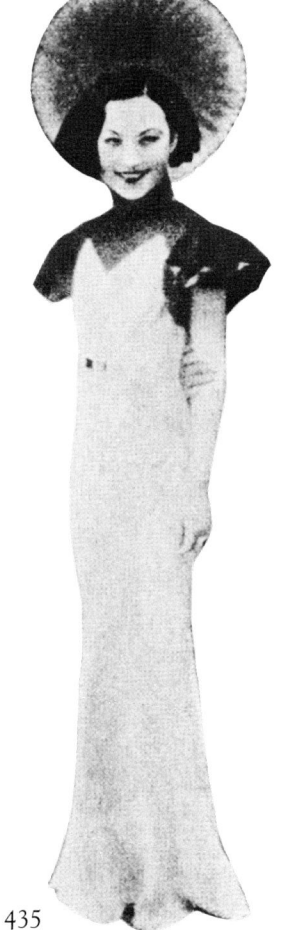

Modern Times 237

433

434

436

437

438

238 Modern Times

6. Costumes of the Common People

Although costumes of the common people in this period were no longer restricted by regulations and taboos, limited income prevented commoners from following the fashions. Ordinarily, men and women wore two-piece garments, as gowns were considered only suitable for such "intellectuals" who made their living by writing letters for others or selling their calligraphic scripts or paintings.

The sleeves of garments worn by ordinary people were generally narrow. To allow freedom of movement, the sleeves of women's costumes were not only narrow at the cuffs, but also comparatively short. Public servants, such as postmen, chauffeurs and drivers, wore uniforms, on which were generally printed Chinese characters saying "China Postal Service" "Highway Service" and so forth, together with a number. Pedlars and craftsmen preferred to wear dark-coloured upper garments and trousers, and almost always wore hats made of felt, cotton, leather or straw. When visiting friends or relatives, some men wore gowns, while women might wear the *qi pao,* but the styles were mostly old-fashioned.

Fig. 439 Women workers in short-sleeved upper garment and trousers (Photograph)

Fig. 440 A woman in jacket and shorts picking water chestnuts (Photograph)

Modern Times 239

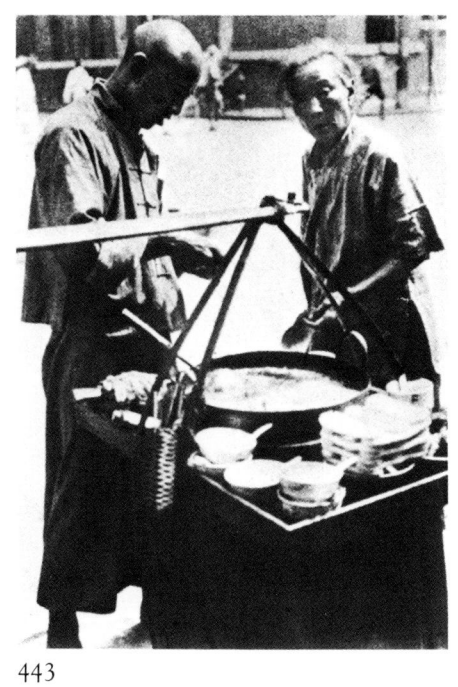

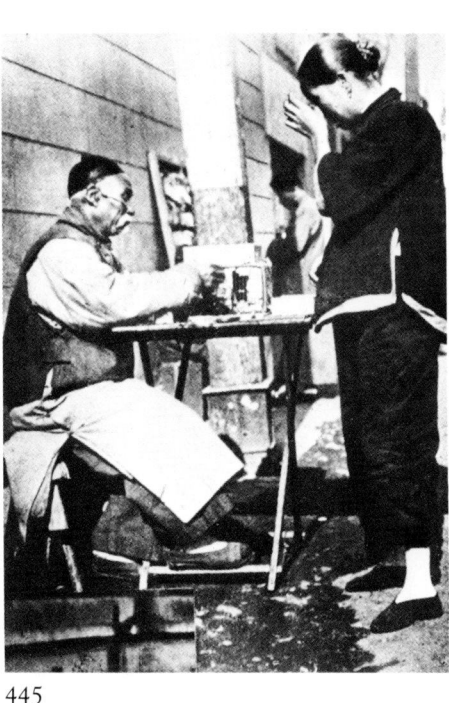

441

442

443

444

445

446

Fig. 441 A lantern pedlar in felt hat and cotton-padded coat with apron (Photograph)

Fig. 442 A fisherwoman in bamboo hat and short-sleeved jacket (Photograph)

Fig. 443 A beancurd float seller in jacket and trousers (Photograph)

Fig. 444 A postman in cotton-padded hat and livery (Photograph)

Fig. 445 A professional letter writer in skull cap and long robe with sleeveless outer jacket (Photograph)

Fig. 446 Two craftsmen, one bare-chested, the other in short jacket and apron (Photograph)

240 Modern Times

7. Jewellery

The jewellery used by women of modern times was derived from traditional forms. The earlier name for an ear-ring was *er dang* (ear ornament of pearl or jade), a necklace was *ying luo* (necklace of precious stone), a bracelet was *tiao tuo* (wrist ornament of jade) and a finger-ring was *zhi huan* (*zhi* for finger and '*huan*' for ring). In China, these articles of jewellery have a history of several thousand years. In primitive society, man started making neck, wrist, hair and chest ornaments out of natural materials, and, with constant improvements over the centuries, these ornaments have always been deeply treasured, especially by women. Different names have been given to such ornaments, to carry different implications. Take the finger ring for example. Historically it has been referred to as *yue zhi* (restriction ring), *ku huan* (shiny ring). *Shou ji* (hand sign), *dai zhi* (substitute), and so on. But *jie zhi* (meaning "avoid touch") was the most commonly used name and has been carried down to the present day. Originally, the ring was not meant for ornament, but was used as a sign of abstention by wives and concubines of emperors. If one of them happened to be pregnant or had another reason for being unable to accept the emperor's love offer, she would put a ring on her finger to signify her abstention. As time went by, the finger ring found its way into the life of common folk and became an ornament for ordinary women. Gradually, its original meaning was lost.

Fig. 447   Finger rings (Actual item)

Fig. 448   Ear ornaments (Actual item)

Fig. 449   A necklace (Actual item)

Fig. 450   A necklace (Actual item)

Fig. 451   Bracelets (Actual item)

Fig. 452   Bracelets (Actual item)

Modern Times 241

449

450

451

452

附錄

APPENDICES

Appendix I Summary Table of Evolution of Costume

Dynasty	Western Zhou	Eastern Zhou	Qin
Year	1100 B.C.-771 B.C.	770 B.C.-221 B.C.	221 B.C.-207 B.C.
Men's Costume			
Characteristics	Narrow-sleeved garment. Large lapel. Large waistband ornamented with axe-shaped knee cover.	Spiral-shaped robe. Large lapel and waistband.	Narrow-sleeved garment. Leather belt. Hook at belt's end. Trousers as lower garment.
Women's Costume			
Characteristics	Narrow-sleeved garment. Rectangular collar. With axe-shaped knee cover below waistband.	Narrow-sleeved garment. Heart-shaped collar. Leather belt with hook.	Narrow-sleeved robe. Collar and sleeves in three folds. Silk waist sash.

Dynasty	Tang	Liao	Song
Year	618-907	916-1125	960-1279
Men's Costume			
Characteristics	Round-collared robe with large lapel. Narrow sleeves. A band below the knees.	Round-collared robe with narrow sleeves. Girdle round the waist with long strips hanging down the knees.	Round-collared robe. Enormous sleeves. A band below the knees.
Women's Costume			
Characteristics	Narrow-sleeved short jacket. Long shirt. Short-sleeved outer upper garment.	Round-collared robe with narrow sleeves. Left opening. Girdle round the waist with long stripes hanging down the knees.	Narrow-sleeved over-dress with front opening. Long skirt as lower garment.

Han	Wei and Jin	Southern and Northern Dynasties	Sui
206 B.C.-220	220-420	420-589	581-618
Spiral-shaped robe. Broad sleeves. Large waistband. Skirt as lower garment.	Large lapel unlined upper garment. Enormous sleeves. Apron round the waist.	Pleated coat and breeches. Outer waistcoat. Trouser legs tied at the knees.	Broad-sleeved garment. Circular collar. Waistcoat outside.
Spiral-shaped robe. Broad sleeves. Lapel spiralling downward. Silk waist sash.	Narrow-sleeved unlined upper garment with embroidered cape. Long skirt as lower garment.	Front-opening unlined upper parment. Loose sleeves. Long skirt as lower garment.	Narrow-sleeved short jacket. Long skirt made to trail on the floor.

Yuan	Ming	Qing	Modern Times
1271-1368	1368-1644	1644-1911	
Large-lapel narrow-sleeved robe made to trail on the floor.	Robe with circular collar. Square patch on mid-front and back. Wide strips under the armpits.	Long gown with horse-shoe sleeves. Slit opened in the middle. Riding jacket with front opening as outer garment.	Riding jacket with front opening over narrow-sleeved long gown.
Large-lapel robe. Sleeves taken in at the cuffs. Made to trail on the floor.	Loose-sleeved unlined upper garment. Long skirt. Sleeveless over-dress.	Large-lapel riding jacket over narrow-sleeved 'qi pao'.	Sleeveless 'qi pao' with silver-ingot-shaped collar. Bottom of garment made to trail on the floor.

Appendix II Illustrations Indicating Specific Parts of Costumes

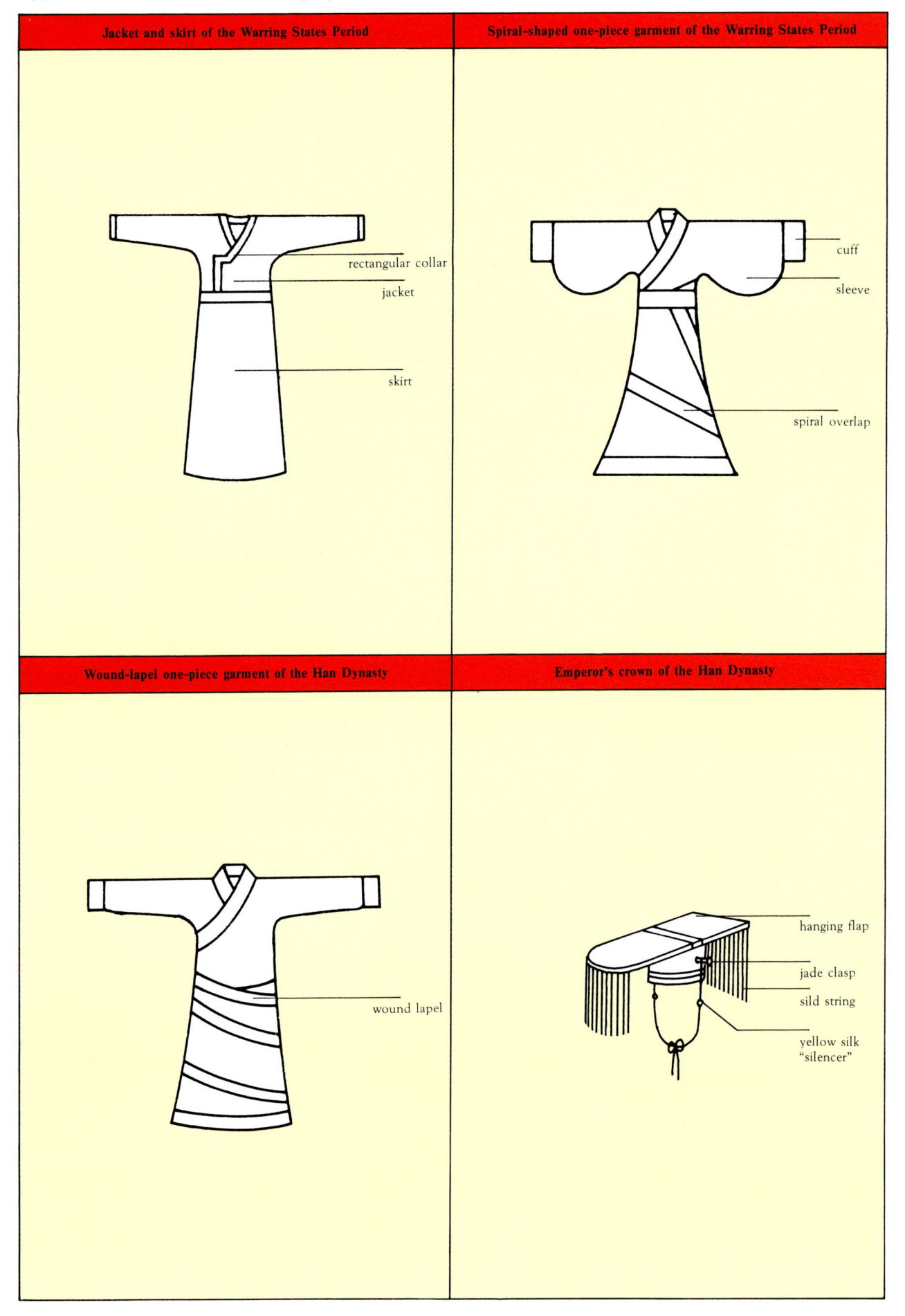

Jacket and skirt of the Warring States Period

- rectangular collar
- jacket
- skirt

Spiral-shaped one-piece garment of the Warring States Period

- cuff
- sleeve
- spiral overlap

Wound-lapel one-piece garment of the Han Dynasty

- wound lapel

Emperor's crown of the Han Dynasty

- hanging flap
- jade clasp
- sild string
- yellow silk "silencer"

Women's multi-lap swallowtail costume	Cage hat of Wei, Jin and the Southern and Northern Dynasties
short-out skirt / "swallow tail" ornament / flying ribbon	cage hat / small hat / hat tassel

Outer waistcoat and fastened breeches of the Northern Dynasty	Large-sleeved gown of the Tang Dynasty
protective plates (chest and back) / leather belt / tied trouser leg	unlined upper garment / cape / shirt

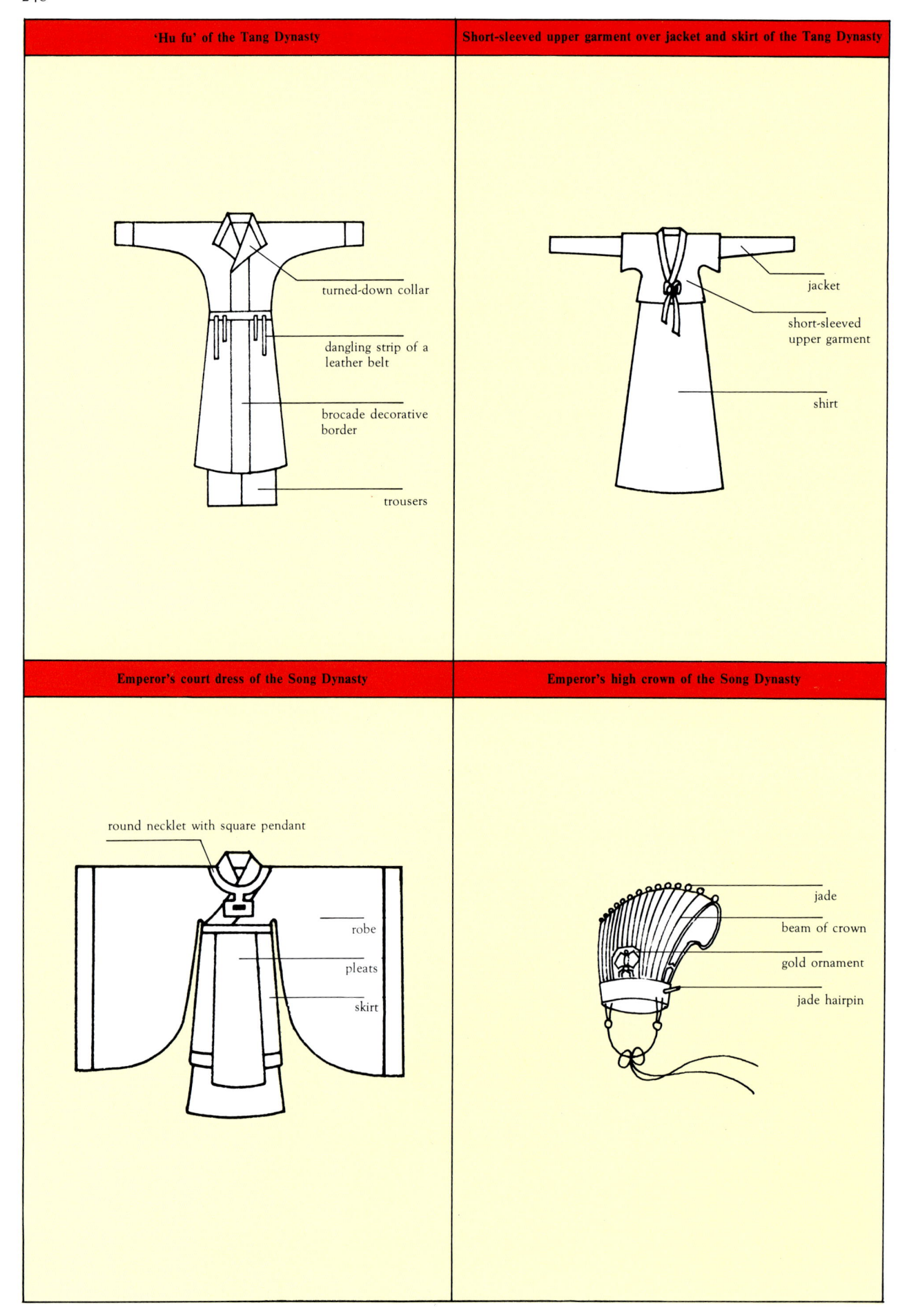

'Hu fu' of the Tang Dynasty	Short-sleeved upper garment over jacket and skirt of the Tang Dynasty
turned-down collar dangling strip of a leather belt brocade decorative border trousers	jacket short-sleeved upper garment shirt
Emperor's court dress of the Song Dynasty	**Emperor's high crown of the Song Dynasty**
round necklet with square pendant robe pleats skirt	jade beam of crown gold ornament jade hairpin

Large girdle of the Song Dynasty

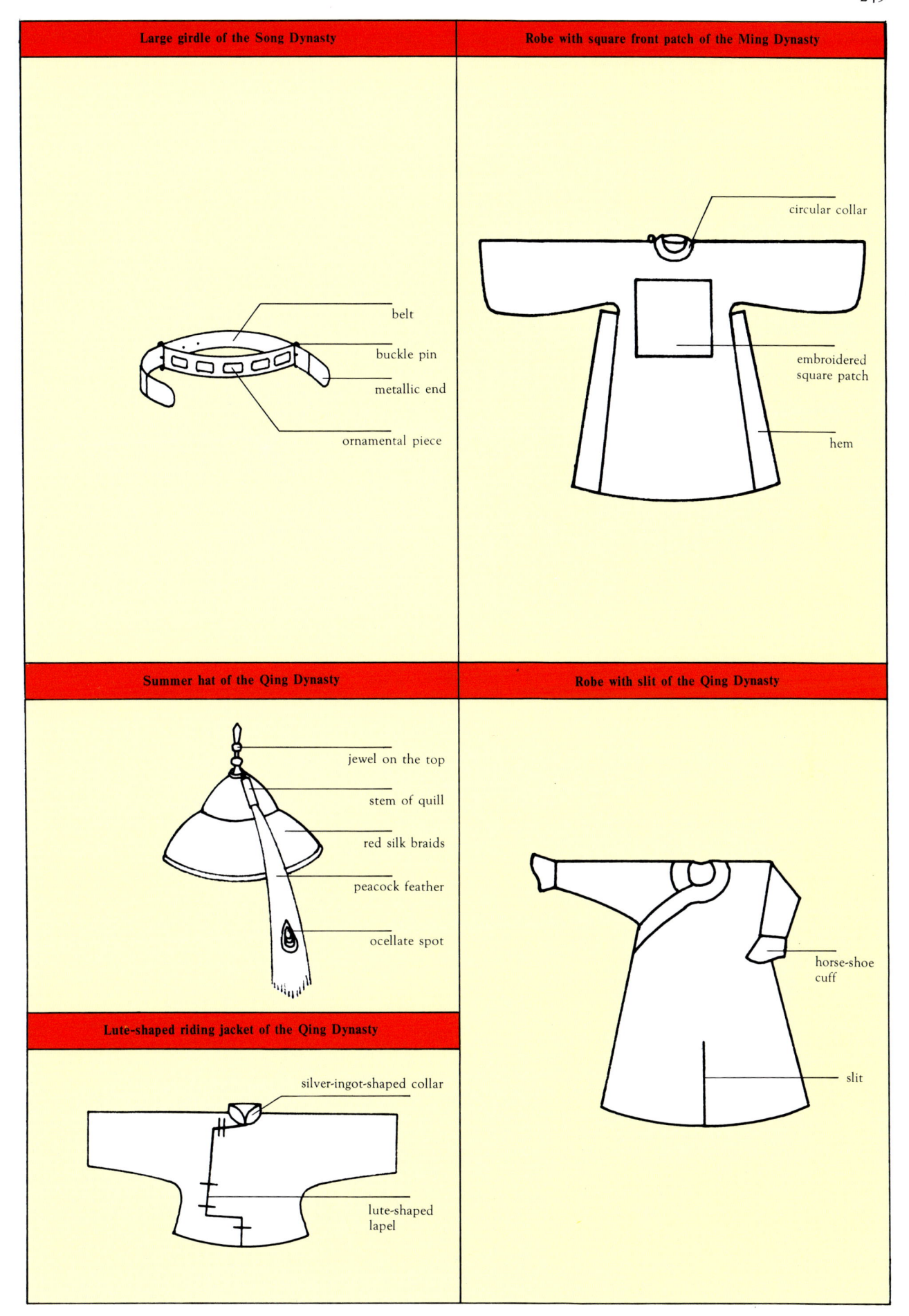

- belt
- buckle pin
- metallic end
- ornamental piece

Robe with square front patch of the Ming Dynasty

- circular collar
- embroidered square patch
- hem

Summer hat of the Qing Dynasty

- jewel on the top
- stem of quill
- red silk braids
- peacock feather
- ocellate spot

Robe with slit of the Qing Dynasty

- horse-shoe cuff
- slit

Lute-shaped riding jacket of the Qing Dynasty

- silver-ingot-shaped collar
- lute-shaped lapel

Appendix III Table Showing Measurements of Spread Illustrations of Costumes

Unit: cm.

Fig. No.	Times	Name of Costume	Size Sleeve span	Size Length	Remarks
1	Ancient Times	Primitive clothing and necklace	54	98	
12		Symmetrically tailored garment with narrow sleeves and embroidered axe-shaped ornament	150	145	including skirt
15		Rectangular collared robe with narrow sleeves	169	138	
16		Spread of a symmetrically patterned garment with narrow sleeves	142	114	
17		Rectangular collared robe with narrow sleeves	178	149	
23		Embroidered silk gauze unlined garment	114	86	
25		Two-piece costume comprising a narrow-sleeved short jacket and a check long skirt	120	141	
26		Spiral-shaped robe	152	164	
30		Wound-lapel one-piece garment with big sleeves	171	165	
33		Women's spiral-shaped garment with narrow sleeves	148	136	
42	Qin and Han	Emperor's 'mian fu'	190	186	including skirt
47		Grey robe with lozenge patterns	168	158	including skirt
53		Spiral-shape one-piece garment	147	132	including skirt
58		Spiral-shape one-piece garment	156	154	including skirt
60		Wound-lapel one-piece garment with narrow sleeves	178	150	
62		Wound-lapel one-piece garment with loose sleeves	158	140	
64		Women's straight robe	208	126	
67		Women's jacket and skirt	174	152	including attached sleeves
68		Dancing costume	202	148	including attached white cuffs
72		Armour for commanding officers of Qin Dynasty	142	156	including trousers
74		Armour for officers and men of Qin Dynasty	148	158	including trousers
75		Armour for ordinary soldiers of Qin Dynasty	178	161	including trousers
76		Armour for commanding officers of Han Dynasty	98	153	span of one sleeve only
78		Armour for ordinary soldiers of Han Dynasty	140	156	including shoes
79		Armour for commanding officers of Han Dynasty	158	158	including boots
85	Wei, Jin and the Southern and Northern Dynasties	Loose gown with large sleeves	178	150	
96		'Ku zhe'	150	156	
98		Women's multi-lap swallowtail costume	165	150	
102		Women's multi-lap swallowtail costume	148	144	
105		Dress style of large-sleeved unlined garment and skirt with spaced colour stripes	126	152	
107		Broad-sleeved upper garment with front opening	154	156	
120		Vest armour	149	162	including trousers
122		Shiny armour	166	163	including trousers
130	Sui, Tang and the Five Dynasties	Large-sleeved ceremonial dress	158	162	including skirt
134		Round-collared robe	170	136	
153		Short jacket, long skirt and cape	136	152	
155		Short jacket, long skirt and overgarment with turned-down collar and narrow sleeves	130	155	
156		Short-sleeved upper garment with low-out collar over jacket and skirt	128	144	
160		Jacket and skirt together with short-sleeved upper garment	130	142	
161		Jacket and skirt with cape	132	149	
164		'Hu fu' with turned-down collar and front opening, striped trousers and leather belt	130	145	
167		Large-sleeved silk gown with front opening, long skirt and cape	144	156	
169		Broad-sleeved gown with front opening, long skirt and cape	138	152	
170		Dancing costume	138	146	
176		Hui Hu costume	150	164	

Fig. No.	Times	Name of Costume	Size		Remarks
			Sleeve span	Length	
180		Armour	82	110	excluding helmet and boots
181	Sui, Tang and the Five Dynasties	Armour	162	159	
185	Song	Crimson gauze robe, knee cover and round necklet with square pendant	192	160	including skirt
186		'Zhong dan'	186	156	
190		Ceremonial dress for the empress	168	146	
192		Official's formal dress	183	162	excluding 'fu tou'
200		Broad-sleeved garment	176	128	
201		Broad-sleeved gown of satin gauze and long skirt	137	145	
204		Broad-sleeved gown with front opening, cape and long skirt	125	142	
208		Over-dress	156	144	including skirt
211		Narrow-sleeved short jacket, long skirt and cape	154	155	
222		Armour	146	156	including boots
225	Liao, Jin and Yuan	Round-collared robe	150	148	including trousers
228		Tight-sleeved robe with left opening	149	141	
233		Round-collared robe with tight sleeves	161	143	
234		Tight-sleeved robe with left opening and long skirt	143	148	
235		Gold brocade dragon robe	178	150	
237		Half-sleeved gold brocade costume	106	155	
239		Plaited garment	188	154	
241		Cross-collared gold brocade robe	158	154	
243		Jacket and skirt and half sleeve over-jacket	124	146	
246	Ming	Dragon robe	185	157	
249		Pheasant garment	148	155	
254		Robe with square front patch for officials of first rank	228	155	
261		Robe embroidered with unicorns	212	121	
269		Large lapel robe adorned with motifs of " 壽 " (longevity) upheld by five bats	220	153	
271		Robe of knitted satin with 'baoxiang' flower and twined branches	183	150	
277		Jacket and skirt	120	136	
279		Jacket and skirt with waist skirt	154	156	
284		Narrow-sleeved over-dress	180	146	including skirt
285		Broad-sleeved over-dress	138	142	including skirt
288		Sleeveless over-dress	45	118	
289		Paddy-field design garment	158	148	
291		Armour worn by commanding officers	155	162	including boots but excluding helmet
295	Qing	Emperor's court robe	198	159	
298		Dragon robe	204	153	
299		Dragon robe	204	153	
302		Court costume	186	158	
304		"Phoenix garment"	152	139	
305		"Hundred-butterfly garment"	143	142	
360		Stage costume — the python robe	292	162	including attached white cuffs
363		Dragon robe of Prince Zhong	202	156	
365		Riding jacket with coiled dragon designs	148	71	
366		Riding jacket with circular floral design	148	70	
367		Women's narrow-sleeved garment	163	145	
368		Women's broad-sleeved garment	148	131	
372		Military uniform	56	115	

Appendix IV Bibliography

The Twenty-Four Histories
Collated Edition, Chung Hwa Book Company

Explanation of Names
(Han) Liu Xi
Collected Series Edition, The Commercial Press

An Analytical Dictionary of Characters
(Han) Xu Shen
Reprint, Chung Hwa Book Company, 1963

Records of the Origins of Affairs and Things
(Song) Gao Cheng
Reprint, The Commercial Press, 1937

An Encyclopaedia of Art and Literature
(Tang) Ouyang Xun, Pei Ju, et al.
Reprint, Chung Hwa Book Company, 1957

The Imperial Encyclopaedia (of Books, Ancient and Modern)
(Qing) Chen Menglei, Revised by Jiang Tingxi et al.
Chung Hwa Book Company, 1934

The Donghua Summary (of the Cabinet Archives of the Qing Dynasty)
(Qing) Jiang Liangqi
Reprint, Chung Hwa Book Company, 1980

Notes from the Materials on the History of Chinese Society
Ju Xuanying
The Commercial Press, 1937

Memoirs of Neglected Matters
(Jin) Wang Jia
Reprint, Chung Hwa Book Company, 1981

Reports on Spiritual Manifestations
(Jin) Gan Bao
Reprint, Chung Hwa Book Company, 1979

New Discourses on the Talk of the Times
(Southern Dynasties) Liu Yiqing
Reprint, Shanghai Chinese Classics Publishing House, 1982

Records of Buddhist Temples in Luoyang
(Later Wei) Yang Xuanzhi
Reprint, The Commercial Press, 1920

Anecdotes of the Sui and Tang Dynasties
(Tang) Liu Su
Reprint, Classical Literature Publishing House, 1957

New Discourses on the Great Tang Dynasty
(Tang) Liu Su
Reprint, Classical Literature Publishing House, 1957

The Youyang Miscellany
(Tang) Tuan Chengshi
Reprint, Chung Hwa Book Company, 1981

Political Records of the Zhenguan Years (of the Tang Dynasty)
(Tang) Wu Jing
Reprint, Shanghai Chinese Classics Publishing House, 1978

Miscellanea of the Tang Dynasty
(Song) Wang Dang
Reprint, Shanghai Chinese Classics Publishing House, 1978

Personal Knowledge of Pictures and Paintings
(Song) Guo Ruoxu
Reprint, The People's Fine Arts Publishing House, 1963

Old Stories of Wulin
(Song) Zhou Mi
Reprint, The West Lake Book Company, Hongzhou, 1981

Memoirs of the Eastern Capital
(Song) Meng Yuanlao
Reprint, Classical Literature Publishing House, 1958

Memoirs of Pianliang
(Song) Wu Zimu
Reprint, The People's Publishing House of Zhejiang, 1980

Five Illustrated Books of Romance
Originally published in the Yuan Dynasty, reprinted by Shanghai Chinese Classics Publishing House, 1955

Miscellanies in Seven Categories
(Ming) Lang Ying
Reprint, Chung Hwa Book Company, 1959

Talks of the Traveller in Chang'an
(Ming) Jiang Yikui
Reprint, Beijing Publishing House, 1960

Anecdotes of the Court in the Wanli Years (of the Ming Dynasty)
(Ming) Shen Defu
Reprint, Chung Hwa Book Company, 1959

Reflections on the Times
(Qing) Ye Mengzhu
Shanghai Chinese Classics Publishing House, 1981

Yangzhou Miscellanies
(Qing) Li Dou
Reprint, Chung Hwa Book Company, 1960

Xiaoting Miscellanies
(Qing) Zhao Lian
Reprint, Chung Hwa Book Company, 1980

A Study of Ancient Chinese Dress
Shen Congwen
The Commercial Press, Hongkong Branch, 1981

Studies in Ancient Chinese Weaponry
Yang Hong
Wenwu Publishing House, 1980

A Short History of the Development of the Chinese New Year Picture
A Ying
Zhao Hua Publishing House, 1954

The Cultures of Chang'an and the Western Regions in the Tang Dynasty
Xiang Da
San Lian Book Company, Beijing, 1957

A Historical Study of Social Customs
Shang Binghe
The Commercial Press, 1938

Guan Tang Miscellanies: A Study of the Costumes of the Northern and Western Tribes in China
Wang Guowei
Reprint, Chung Hwa Book Company, 1959

A Study of the Confucian Scholars' Costumes
Qi Sihe
in *The Annual of Historical Studies* No. 2, 1930

"Deep Dress" and the Chu Costume
Sun Ji
in *Archaeology and Cultural Relics* No. 1, 1982

A Manual of Bureaucratic Systems and Official Titles of All the Dynasties
(Qing) Huang Bengji
Reprint, Chung Hwa Book Company, 1965

A Picture Album of the Rules and Measuring Tools of All Ages
Luo Fuyi
Wenwu Publishing House, 1957

Thirty Years' Work on Cultural Relics and Archaeology
Wenwu Editorial Board
Wenwu Publishing House, 1979

The Achievements in Archaeological Research in New China
Archaeological Research Institute, Academia Sinica, Wenwu Publishing House, 1961

Reports on the Excavations at Huixian
Archaeological Research Institute, Academia Sinica, Science Publishing House, Beijing, 1956

A Report on the Excavation of the Han Tomb at Mancheng
The Cultural Relics Management Office of Hebei Province Wenwu Publishing House, 1980

A Report on the Excavation of the Ancient Tomb with the Stone Relief at Yinan
Nanjing Museum and the Cultural Relics Management Office of Shandong Province
The Cultural Relics Administrative Bureau of the Ministry of Cultural Affairs, 1956

Reports on the Excavations at Changsha
The Archaeological Research Institute, Academia Sinica, Beijing Science Publising House, 1957

Reports on the Excavations at Fengxi
The Archaeological Research Institute, Academia Sinica, Wenwu, Publishing House, 1963

A Report on the Excavation of the Mausoleum of Wang Jian of the Former Shu
Feng Hanji
Wenwu Publishing House, 1964

A Report on the Excavation of the Two Mausoleums of South Tang
Wanjing Museum
Wenwu Publishing House, 1957

A Book of the Selected Unearthed Artifacts of Jiangsu Province
Nanjing Museum
Wenwu Publishing House, 1963

A Book of the Selected Unearthed Artifacts of Nei Monggol (Inner Mongolia)
The Work Team for Cultural Relics of the Nei Monggol Autonomous Region
Wenwu Publishing House, 1963

A Picture Album of the Important Unearthed Artifacts of the Five Provinces Exhibited
The Preparatory Committee for the Exhibition of the Important Unearthed Artifacts of the Five Provinces
Wenwu Publishing House, 1958

A Picture Album of the Artifacts Unearthed from the Tomb of Zhang Su of North Qi at Kuangpi, Taiyuan
Shanxi Museum
Chinese Classical Art Publishing House, Beijing, 1958

A Picture Album of the Cultural Relics in Hunan Province
Hunan Museum
The People's Publishing House of Hunan, 1964

The Unearthed Artifacts of Xinjiang Province
The Museum of the Xinjiang Uygur Autonomous Region
Wenwu Publishing House, 1975

The Silk Road – The Textiles of the Han and Tang Dynasties
The Work Team for the Exhibition of the Unearthed Artifacts, the Museum of the Xinjiang Uygut Autonomous Region
Wenwu Publishing House, 1972

Jade Artifacts Unearthed at Yinxu
The Archaeological Research Institute, Academia Sinica, Wenwu Publishing House, 1982

The Tri-coloured Glazed Pottery of the Tang Dynasty at Luoyang
Luoyang Museum
Wenwu Publishing House, 1980

The Tombs of the Sui and Tang Period in the Suburbs of Chang'an of the Tang Dynasty
The Archaeological Research Institute, Academia Sinica, Wenwu Publishing House, 1980

Chinese Pottery and Porcelain
Tan Danjiong
Guan Fu Book Co., Ltd., Taibei, 1980

A Picture Album of Chinese Pottery and Porcelain
Zuo Yide
Ji Wen Book Company, Taibei, 1977

The Jin Ancestral Hall
Taiyuan Management Committee for Cultural Relics and the Office for the Reservation of the Jin Ancestral Hall of Shanxi Wenwu Publishing House, 1981

The Dress of the Han and the Six Dynasties
Yoshito Harada, 1937

The Dress of the Tang Dynasty
Yoshito Harada, 1970

Chinese Fine Arts
Yu Sekino and Buraku Nagatani, Kodansha, Tokyo, 1978

The Fine Arts of the Sui and Tang Dynasties
The Municipal Art Gallery of Osaka
Heibonsha, Tokyo, 1978

An Illustrated History of China
Gantaro Ando et al.
Kodansha, Tokyo, 1976

Shosoin and the Arts and Crafts of the Tang Dynasty
Hiroshi Abe
Heibonsha, Tokyo, 1981

The Gaojuli Frescoes
The Foreign Languages Publishing House of Pyongyong, Korea, 1958

China and Its People (An Pictorial published in England)
Periodicals published before 1949:

Beiyang Pictorial
The Popular Pictorial
Liangyou Pictorial
Shanghai Pictorial
Women's Pictorial
Qingqing
Linglong, etc

Periodicals published since 1949:

The People's Pictorial
The National Pictorial
Reference Materials Concerning Cultural Relics
Wenwu (Cultural Relics)
Kaoku (Archaeology)
The Journal of Archaeological Research

Appendix V Index of Figures

Figure

Ancient Times

1	Primitive clothing and necklace	14
2,3	Two views of a braid	15
4,5	Shang Dynasty men, braid coiled up on top	15
6	A Shang Dynasty woman wearing a hairpin	16
7	Jade hairpins of the Shang Dynasty	16
8,9	Bone hairpins of the Shang Dynasty	16
10	A Shang Dynasty man wearing a hairpin	17
11	Rear view of a Shang Dynasty man wearing a head band	17
12	Symmetrically tailored garment with narrow sleeves and embroidered axe-shaped ornament	18
13	Nobleman wearing cylinder-shaped cap and narrow-sleeved costume with embroidered axe-shaped ornament	18
14	Nobleman wearing cylinder-shaped cap and elaborate garment	18
15	Rectangular collared robe with narrow sleeves	19
16	Spread of a symmetrically patterned garment with narrow sleeves	20
17	Rectangular collared robe with narrow sleeves	21
18	Male figure in cap and rectangular collared robe with narrow sleeves	22
19	A king's bodyguard in rectangular collared outfit with narrow sleeves	22
20-22	Gold and silver interlocking hooks	22
23	Embroidered silk gauze unlined garment	23
24	Embroidery design	23
25	Two-piece costume comprising a narrow-sleeved short jacket and a check long skirt	24
26	Spiral-shape robe	25
27	Robed female in the State of Chu	25
28	A servant in 'shenyi' with big sleeves and wound lapel	26
29	A nobleman in high hat and long robe	26
30	Spread of wound-lapel one-piece garment with big sleeves	26
31	Male figures of the Warring States Period wearing spiral-shaped one-piece garment with wound lapel	26
32	A nobleman dressed in spiral-shaped garment with wound lapel and colour embroidery	26
33	Women's spiral-shaped costume with narrow sleeves	27
34	Women in spiral-shaped one-piece garment with narrow sleeves	27
35	Bronze 'dou wu' of the Warring States Period	28
36	Iron 'dou wu' of the Warring States Period	28
37	Warriors' outfit in the Warring States Period	28
38	Male figure in cap and narrow-sleeved gown reaching the knees	29
39	A servant wearing narrow-sleeved jacket	29
40	Acrobat in narrow-sleeved jacket	29
41	A Warring States Period woman, double-braided and wearing 'hu fu'	29

Qin and Han Dynasties

42	Emperor's 'mian fu'	34
43	Emperor's 'mian guan'	34
44	Emperor's 'chi xi'	34
45,46	Officials in 'mian guan'	35
47	Grey robe with lozenge patterns	36
48	A male-servant in gown and kerchief	36
49	An official in 'liang guan' and robe	36
50	An official in 'liang guan' and robe	37
51	An official in 'liang guan' and robe and wearing brush hairpin	37
52	A civil official in 'jin xian guan' and robe	37
53	Spiral-shaped one-piece garment	38
54	Male figure in spiral-shaped one-piece garment	38
55-57	Male figures in hat and spiral shaped one-piece garment	39
58	Spiral-shaped one-piece garment	40
59	A woman in spiral-shaped one-piece garment	40
60	Wound-lapel one-piece garment with narrow sleeves	41
61	Servants in 'chang guan' and wound-lapel one-piece garment with narrow sleeves	41
62	Wound-lapel one-piece garment with loose sleeves	42
63	A woman in wound-lapel one-piece garment with loose sleeves	42
64	Women's straight robe	43
65	A woman in straight robe	43
66	Printed crimson silk straight robe	43
67	Women's jacket and skirt	44
68	Dancing costume	45
69	A female dancer in dancing costume	45
70	A female dancer in long-sleeved dancing costume	46
71	Female dancers in long-sleeved dancing costume and wearing swallow-tail bun	46
72,73	Armour for commanding officers of Qin Dynasty	47
74	Armour for officers and men of Qin Dynasty	48
75	Armour for ordinary soldiers of Qin Dynasty	48
76,77	Armour for commanding officers of Han Dynasty	49
78	Armour for ordinary soldiers of Han Dynasty	50
79,80	Armour for commanding officers of Han Dynasty	50
81-84	Officers and men of Qin Dynasty clad in armour	51

Wei, Jin and the Southern and Northern Dynasties

85	Loose gown with large sleeves	56
86	Lacquered gauze cage hat	56
87	A monarch in a water-chestnut-shaped kerchief and large-sleeved gown	57
88	Aristocrats in loose gowns with large sleeves escorted by their attendants	57
89	A nobleman in curled beam hat and robe	58
90	An aristocrat in curled beam hat and large-sleeved gown. His attendant in cage hat and gown	58
91	A nobleman in cage hat and large-sleeved gown	58
92,93	Scholars in small hat or kerchief and loose gown	59
94	Scholars in kerchiefs with gowns draped over their shoulders	60
95	A scholar in kerchief and loose gown	60
96	'Ku zhe'	61
97	A man in 'ku zhe'	61
98	Women's multi-lap swallowtail costume	62
99	A woman in multi-lap swallowtail costume	62
100,101	Women in multi-lap swallowtail costumes	63
102	Women's multi-lap swallowtail costume	64
103	Women in multi-lap swallowtail costume	64
104	Women in multi-lap swallowtail costume	64
105	Dress style of large-sleeved unlined garment and skirt with spaced colour stripes	65
106	An aristocratic woman in large-sleeved unlined garment and skirt with spaced colour stripes, and accompanied by her attendants	65
107	Dress style of broad-sleeved upper garment with front opening and long skirt	66
108	A woman in unlined upper garment with front opening and long skirt	66
109	Woman in unlined upper garment and skirt	67
110	A messenger in turban and robe	68
111	A woman in robe and apron picking mulberry leaves	68
112	A farmer and his wife wearing robes	68
113	A hunter in felt hat and robe	68
114	Musicians in small hats, short jackets and skirts	69
115	A man in a garment with front opening, narrow sleeves and low-cut v-neck	69
116	A woman in hat and wearing jacket and skirt	69
117	A servant in cage hat and wearing jacket and skirt	69
118	A warrior in helmet and tube-sleeve armour	70
119	A warrior in helmet and tube-sleeve armour	70
120	Dress style of the vest armour	71
121	Warriors in helmets and vest armour	71
122	Dress style of the "shiny armour"	72
123	Brocade with pattern of incarnation of celestial ruler	73
124	Embroidered portrait of Buddha	73
125	Brocade with pattern of the one-legged dragon-like monster	73
126	Embroidered decorative border	73
127	Brocade with patterns of animals within square frames	73

Sui, Tang and the Five Dynasties

128	An emperor in crown and official costume accompanied by his attendants	78
129	An emperor in crown and official costume with his attendants in caged hats and ceremonial clothes	78
130	Large-sleeved ceremonial dress	79
131,133	Early Tang civil officials in turbans and large-sleeved gowns	80
132	Civil officials in lacquered gauze cage hats and large-sleeved ceremonial dresses	80
134	The round-collared robe	81
135	The gauze 'fu tou'	81
136	An emperor in 'fu tou' and round-collared robe with his attendants	82
137	Officials in 'fu tou', round-collared robes and black leather boots	83
138	A late Tang official in 'fu tou' and literary robe	82
139	Officials in 'fu tou' and round-collared robes	82
140	A late Tang scholar in stiff-cornered 'fu tou' and literary robe	83
141	A late Tang scholar in stiff-cornered 'fu tou' and literary robe	83
142	Women's bun in the Sui Dynasty	84
143	Women's bun of mid Tang Dynasty	84
144	Women's bun in the heyday of the Tang period	84
145	Women's bun in the heyday of the Tang period	85
146	Women's bun of early Tang Dynasty	85
147	Women's bun of the Five Dynasties	85
148	A woman with 'hua dian' decoration	86
149	Tender-willow eyebrows	86
150	A woman with 'mian ye' on her cheek	87
151	A woman with 'dai mei' eyebrows	87
152	A woman with 'mian ye' on her cheek	87
153	Short jacket, long skirt and cape	88
154	A woman of Sui Dynasty in narrow-sleeved short jacket and long skirt	88
155	Short jacket, long skirt and overgarment with turn-down collar and narrow wleeves	89
156	Short-sleeved upper garment with low-cut collar over jacket and skirt	90
157-159	Women in jacket and skirt, short-sleeved upper garment and cape	91
160	Jacket and skirt together with short-sleeved upper garment	91
161	Jacket and skirt with cape	92
162	A woman in short jacket and skirt together with cape	92
163	A woman in jacket and skirt together with cape	92
164	'Hu fu' with turn-down collar and front opening, striped trousers and leather belt	93
165	A woman in 'hu fu' and Tartar hat	93
166	A woman in 'hu fu' with turn-down collar and wearing a bun	93
167	Dress style of large-sleeved silk gown with front opening, long skirt and cape	94
168	An aristocratic woman in large-sleeved silk gown with long skirt and cape	94
169	Dress style of broad-sleeved gown with front opening, long skirt and cape	95
170	Dancing costume	96
171	A woman in dancing costume	96
172	A woman in dancing costume	97
173	A woman in dancing costume	97
174	A woman in dancing costume	97
175	Women in dancing costumes	97
176	Hui Hu costume	98
177	A late Tang aristocratic woman in Hui Hu bun, a golden phoenix hat and Hui Hu costume	99
178	A variant of the treasure-patterned brocade shoes with toe caps shaped in cloud patterns	99
179	A warrior in helmet and coat of mail	100
180	Dress style of helmet, coat of mail, and boots	100
181	Dress style of helmet and coat of mail	101
182	A Tang warrior in silk armour	102
183	A cavalryman in full armour	103
184	Imperial guards in embroidered robes	103

Song Dynasty

185	Crimson gauze robe, knee cover and round necklet with square pendant	108
186	'Zhong dan'	109
187	The high crown	108
188	The black boots	109
189	An emperor in high crown, crimson gauze robe and round necklet with square pendant	109
190	Ceremonial dress for the empress	110
191	An empress wearing a dragon-phoenix crown adorned with pearls and emeralds	110
192	Official's formal dress; turban cap with outstretched "feet"; and large girdle with jade embellishments	111
193	An official in soft "feet" turban cap and round-collared robe	112
194	White unlined gown with round collar	112
195	Lacquered gauze 'fu tou'	113
196	Silk shoes with patterns of water caltrops	113
197	Lined jacket with front opening and embellished with a peony flower and twisted branch	113
198	A scholar in turban and gown	114
199	White gauze unlined garment with front opening	114
200	Broad-sleeved garment	115
201	Broad-sleeved gown of satin gauze and long skirt	116
202	A woman in phoenix crown, gown and skirt, wearing pendant	116
203	Gold hairpin with phoenix head	116
204	Broad-sleeved gown with front opening, cape and long skirt	117
205	Aristocratic women in coronet-comb, broad-sleeved gown, long skirt and cape	117
206	White satin gauze broad-sleeved garment	118
207	Part of white satin gauze broad-sleeved garment	118
208	Over-dress	119
209	Women in over-dress	119
210	Over-dress made from crepe fabric	120
211	Narrow-sleeved short jacket, long skirt and cape	121
212	Women wearing hairpins, short jacket and skirt, and cape	121
213	Aristocratic women wearing hairpins, short jackets and skirts, and capes, served by a maid dressed in a gown	122
214	A maid of honour in short jacket with narrow sleeves	122
215	A maid of honour in jacket and skirt, with cape	122
216	A maid of honour in jacket and skirt, with cape, and wearing jade pendant	122
217	Pleated skirt made of printed satin gauze	123
218	Skirt with hem fringed with satin borders	123
219,220	Common people in various costumes	124
221	Peasants in head scarves, wearing jackets and trousers	125
222	A suit of armour	126
223	A warrior in full armour	127
224	Warriors in full armour	127

Liao, Jin and Yuan Dynasties

225	Round-collared robe	132
226	Khitan horsemen in round-collared robe	133
227	Hair-shaved Khitan aristocrats wearing round-collared robes with tight sleeves	133
228	Tight-sleeved robe with left opening	134
229	Khitan women in tight-sleeved robes with left opening and men in round-collared robes	134
230	Horsemen in round-collared robes	135
231,232	Khitan men and women in tight-sleeved robes	135
233	Round-collared robe with tight sleeves	136
234	Dress style of tight-sleeved robe with left opening and long skirt	137
235	Gold brocade dragon robe, palm hat, cloud-patterned cape and satin boot	138
236	Emperor in fur and attendants in gold brocade	138
237	Half-sleeved gold brocade costume	139
238	An aristocrat in headwear and gold brocade robe	139
239	Plaited garment, square corrugated hat and leather boot	140
240	A man in corrugated hat and plaited garment	140

Appendix V Index of Figures

241	Cross-collared gold brocade robe	141
242	An empress in 'gu gu guan' and cross-collared gold brocade robe	141
243,244	Jacket and skirt and half sleeve over-jacket — front and rear views	142
245	A maid in a colourfully decorated hat, jacket and skirt, and half sleeve over-jacket	143

Ming Dynasty

246	Dragon robe	148
247	Gold crown with turn-up turban	148
248	An emperor in circular-collared robe with narrow sleeves	149
249	Pheasant garment	150
250	Knee cover	150
251	Rosy cape	150
252	Empress' dragon and phoenix crown adorned with pearls and emeralds	151
253	An empress in phoenix crown and rosy cape	151
254	Robe with square front patch for officials of first rank	152
255	A Ming Dynasty official in black gauze cap and circular-collared robe with front patch	153
256	Black gauze cap	153
257,258	Square patches embroidered with 'xi li' for civil officials of seventh rank	154
259,260	Square patches embroidered with orioles on front and back pieces of the same robe	154
261	A robe embroidered with unicorns	155
262	An official in black gauze 'fu tou' and robe with pattern of python embroidered in gold	155
263	Hair-tying jade coronet	155
264	Jade buckle and hook	155
265	Jade hairpins	155
266	Broad-sleeved robe	156
267	Broad-sleeved robe	156
268	Broad-sleeved robe	157
269	Large lapel robe adorned with motifs of " 壽 " (longevity) upheld by five bats	158
270	A man in quadrangular flat-topped turban and large-lapel robe	158
271	Robe of knitted satin with 'baowiang' flower and twined branches	158
272,273	Round-collared upper garment with broad sleeves	159
274	Turban for scholars	160
275	High felt boots	160
276	Square turban	160
277	Jacket and skirt	161
278	Women musicians in jackets and skirts	161
279	Jacket and skirt with waist skirt	162
280	Attending maids in jackets and skirts	162
281	A jacket	163
282	A skirt	163
283	A noblewoman and attending maids in narrow-sleeved over-dress	164
284	Narrow-sleeved over-dress	164
285	Broad-sleeved over-dress	165
286	A noblewoman in broad-sleeved over-dress	165
287	A woman wearing sleeveless over-dress	166
288	Sleeveless over-dress	166
289	Dress style of paddy-field design garment	167
290	A woman in paddy-field design dress	167
291	Dress style of suit of armour worn by commanding officers	168
292	A military officer in full armour	169
293	Helmet	169
294	Warrior in full armour	169

Qing Dynasty

295	Emperor's court robe	174
296	An emperor wearing court crown and court robe	175
297	Court boots	175
298	Dragon robe — front view	176
299	Dragon robe — rear view	177
300	Court hat	178
301	An empress in court hat and robe	178
302	Court costume	179
303	Court over-jacket	179
304	Empress' ordinary dress — "phoenix garment"	180
305	Empress' ordinary dress — "hundred-butterfly garment"	180
306	An empress dowager in ordinary dress	181
307	High sole shoes	181
308	Court robe embroidered with pythons	182
309	Plain court robe with golden borders — rear view	183
310	Over-collar	182
311	Summer hat	184
312	Winter hat	184
313	Hollow stems of quills	184
314	Robe with round patches of coiled dragons	185
315	One of emperor's close relatives in winter hat and robe with round embroidered patches, wearing a necklace	185
316	Jewels for ornamenting top of hats	185
317	A necklace	185
318	Embroidered patch for 1st rank civil official — crane	186
319	Embroidered patch for 2nd rank civil official — golden pheasant	186
320	Embroidered patch for 3rd rank civil official — peacock	186
321	Embroidered patch for 4th rank civil official — wild goose	187
322	Embroidered patch for 5th rank civil official — lophura	187
323	Embroidered patch for 6th rank civil official — egret	187
324	Embroidered patch for 7th rank civil official — violet mandarin duck	187
325	Embroidered patch for 8th rank civil official — quail	187
326	Embroidered patch for 9th rank civil official — long-tailed flycatcher	187
327	Embroidered patch for a prince — coiled dragon	188
328	Embroidered patch for 4th rank military officer — tiger	188
329	Embroidered patch for 3rd rank military officer — leopard	188
330	A civil official in robe with embroidered square patch	188
331	A Qing Dynasty military officer in robe with embroidered patch	188
332	Python robe	189
333	An official in python robe	189
334	Python robe	190
335	Robe with lute-shaped lapel — travelling outfit	191
336	Riding jacket with lute-shaped lapel	191
337	A man in ordinary dress and wearing ornaments	192
338	An official wearing riding jacket and robe	192
339	'Da lian' (pouch worn at the girdle)	193
340	'Da lian' (pouch worn at the girdle)	193
341	Heart-shaped purses	193
342	Cases for folding fans	193
343	A Qing titled lady in phoenix coronet, cloud-patterned scarf and embroidered rosy cape	194
344	Phoenix coronet	194
345	Embroidered rosy cape	194
346	Cloud-patterned scarf	194
347	Low-collared lined upper garment rimmed with decorative designs	195
348	Pleated horse-face skirt made of purple satin	195
349	Embroidered flannelette lined upper garment with buttons down the front	196
350	Narrow-sleeved lined upper garment with decorative borders	196
351	Loose-sleeved floral satin lined upper garment with broad decorative borders	197
352	Narrow-sleeved floral satin lined upper garment with broad decorative borders	197
353	Embroidered brocade cloak	198
354	Vest with lute-shaped lapel	199
355	A woman in Manchu hat, long gown and outer vest	199
356	Armour for military commanders	200
357	Armour for military commanders — rear view	201
358	A military officer in helmet and armour	201
359	Helmet	201
360	Stage costume — python robe	202

Fig.	Description	Page
361, 362	Court crown of Prince Zhong — front and profile	203
363	Dragon robe of Prince Zhong	204
364	Prince Zhong in court crown and dragon robe with his generals in hoop-shaped hats and robes	204
365	Riding jacket with coiled dragon designs	205
366	Riding jacket with circular floral design	205
367	Women's narrow-sleeved garment	206
368	Women's broad-sleeved garment	207
369	A woman of Taiping Heavenly Kingdom in narrow-sleeved garment with left opening	207
370, 371	'Hao mao' (army caps) — front and profile	208
372, 373	Military uniform — front and profile	209
374	An imitation of ancient brocade	210
375	The "hundred sons" brocade	210
376, 377	Samples of decorative borders	211

Modern Times

Fig.	Description	Page
378	'Ma gua' (ceremonial jacket) with front opening and round patterns	216
379	Flannelette jacquard long gown with patterns of pine and crane	216
380	Western style hat	216
381	A man in western style hat, long gown and 'ma gua'	216
382-384	Hairstyles in the early days of the Republic	217
385	Women's hairstyles in 1920's	218
386, 387	Women's hairstyles in 1920's	219
388, 389	Women's hairstyles in 1930's	219
390	The weeping willow bang	220
391	The one-line bang	220
392	The swallow-tail bang	220
393	The "star-studded sky" bun	220
394	Long lined upper garment with high collar and narrow sleeves	221
395	"Horse face" skirt	221
396	High-collared red lined silk garment embroidered with silver flowers	222
397	High-collared lined garment with embroidered patterns	222
398	A woman in high-collared long lined garment with narrow sleeves	222
399	Curve-edged short lined garment with broad sleeves	223
400	Embroidered long red skirt	223
401	A woman in curve-edged short lined garment with broad sleeves and embroidered long skirt	223
402	Illustration of lined upper garment and skirt ensemble	224
403	Embroidered satin short lined upper garment edged with pearls	225
404	Embroidered satin short lined upper garment edged with pearls	225
405	Embroidered slip-on satin skirt edged with shiny borders	226
406	Embroidered slip-on satin skirt	226
407	Short lined upper garment with front opening and shining decorative borders	227
408	Lined upper garment and skirt with shiny decorative borders	227
409	Embroidered satin 'qi pao' with broad decorative borders	228
410	Manchu costume at end of Qing Dynasty and beginning of the Republic	229
411	A woman in long-sleeved 'qi pao' with wavy decorative borders	229
412	A woman in flowered satin 'qi pao' with medium-length sleeves	229
413	A woman in check patterns 'qi pao' with medium-length sleeves	229
414	A woman in short-sleeved 'qi pao' of flowered satin	230
415	A woman in plain short-sleeved 'qi pao'	230
416	A woman in sleeveless 'qi pao' of striped satin	230
417	A woman in sleeveless 'qi pao'	230
418	A woman in modified 'qi pao'	230
419	A woman in 'qi pao' of flowered satin	230
420, 421	Embroidered 'qi pao' made of flowered satin	231
422	'Qi pao' with coloured embroidery and broad decorative borders — fashion of Manchu women in Qing Dynasty	232
423	Long-sleeved 'qi pao' with side opening and coloured embroidery — fashion in early 1920's	232
424	High-collared 'qi pao' with medium-length shoes embroidered with silver cloud-and-dragon patterns — fashion of the mid 1920's	233
425	Long-sleeved 'qi pao' with side opening and coloured embroidery — fashion in late 1920's	233
426	Close-fitting sleeveless 'qi pao' with slit in front — fashion of the early 1930's	234
427	'qi pao' with shoulder pads, attached sleeves and flowery patterns — fashion of the late 1930's	234
428	Sleeveless tapestry satin 'qi pao' with v-shaped opening — fashion in late 1930's	235
429	A woman in short-sleeved mesh 'qi pao'	235
430	Short-sleeved mesh 'qi pao'	235
431	A woman in 'qi pao' and cape	236
432	A woman in short-sleeved dress with turn-down collar	236
433	A woman in 'qi pao' with sleeves shaped like lotus leaves	237
434	A woman in 'qi pao' and bow tie	237
435	A woman in western-style evening dress	236
436	A woman in 'qi pao' and short-sleeved jacket	237
437	A woman in short-sleeved dress	237
438	A woman in western-styled evening dress	237
439	Women workers in short-sleeved upper garment and trousers	238
440	A woman in jacket and shorts picking water chestnuts	238
441	A lantern pedlar in felt hat and cotton-padded coat with apron	239
442	A fisherwoman in bamboo hat and short-sleeved jacket	239
443	A beancurd float seller in jacket and trousers	239
444	A postman in cotton-padded hat and livery	239
445	A professional letter writer in skull cap and long robe with sleeveless outer jacket	239
446	Two craftsmen, one bare-chested, the other in short jacket and apron	239
447	Finger rings	240
448	Ear ornaments	240
449	A necklace	241
450	A necklace	241
451	Bracelets	241
452	Bracelets	241